Geographies of Journalism

Geographies of Journalism connects theoretical and practical discussions of the role of geotechnologies, social media, and boots-on-the-ground journalism in a digital age to underline the complications and challenges that place-making in the press brings to institutions and ideologies. By introducing and applying approaches to geography, cultural resistance, and power as it relates to discussions of space and place, this book takes a critical look at how online news media shapes perceptions of locales. Through verisimilitude, storytelling methods, and journalistic evidence shaped by sources and news processes, the press play a critical role in how audiences shape interpretations of social conditions "here" and "there," and place responsibility for socio-political issues that appear in everyday life.

Issues of proximity, place, territory, news myth, place-making, and power align in this book of innovative and new assessments of journalism in the digital age. This is a valuable resource for scholars across the fields of human geography, journalism, and mass media.

Robert E. Gutsche, Jr. is Senior Lecturer in Critical Digital Media Practice at Lancaster University, UK. His scholarship surrounds place-making in news as imposing social control. He is an author and editor of several books, including *The Trump Presidency, Journalism, and Democracy* (2018).

Kristy Hess is an academic of Journalism and Communications Studies at Deakin University, Australia. She is largely interested in researching the sustainability of local media in a digital era and its connection to place-making, boundary work, and power.

Disruptions: Studies in Digital Journalism
Series editor: Bob Franklin

Disruptions refers to the radical changes provoked by the affordances of digital technologies that occur at a pace and on a scale that disrupts settled understandings and traditional ways of creating value, interacting, and communicating both socially and professionally. The consequences for digital journalism involve far reaching changes to business models, professional practices, roles, ethics, products, and even challenges to the accepted definitions and understandings of journalism. For Digital Journalism Studies, the field of academic inquiry which explores and examines digital journalism, disruption results in paradigmatic and tectonic shifts in scholarly concerns. It prompts reconsideration of research methods, theoretical analyses, and responses (oppositional and consensual) to such changes, which have been described as being akin to "a moment of mind blowing uncertainty."

Routledge's new book series, *Disruptions: Studies in Digital Journalism*, seeks to capture, examine, and analyze these moments of exciting and explosive professional and scholarly innovation which characterize developments in the day-to-day practice of journalism in an age of digital media, and which are articulated in the newly emerging academic discipline of Digital Journalism Studies.

Native Advertising
Lisa Lynch

Geographies of Journalism
The Imaginative Power of Place in Making Digital News
Robert E. Gutsche, Jr. and Kristy Hess

Disrupting Journalism Ethics
Stephen J. A. Ward

www.routledge.com/Disruptions/book-series/DISRUPTDIGJOUR

Geographies of Journalism
The Imaginative Power of Place in
Making Digital News

**Robert E. Gutsche, Jr. and
Kristy Hess**

LONDON AND NEW YORK

First published 2019
by Routledge
2 Park Square, Milton Park, Abingdon, Oxon OX14 4RN

and by Routledge
711 Third Avenue, New York, NY 10017

Routledge is an imprint of the Taylor & Francis Group, an informa business

© 2019 Robert E. Gutsche, Jr. and Kristy Hess

The right of Robert E. Gutsche, Jr. and Kristy Hess to be identified
as authors of this work has been asserted by them in accordance
with sections 77 and 78 of the Copyright, Designs and Patents Act
1988.

All rights reserved. No part of this book may be reprinted
or reproduced or utilised in any form or by any electronic,
mechanical, or other means, now known or hereafter invented,
including photocopying and recording, or in any information
storage or retrieval system, without permission in writing from the
publishers.

Trademark notice: Product or corporate names may be trademarks
or registered trademarks, and are used only for identification and
explanation without intent to infringe.

British Library Cataloguing-in-Publication Data
A catalogue record for this book is available from the British Library

Library of Congress Cataloging-in-Publication Data
Names: Gutsche, Robert E., Jr., 1980– author. | Hess, Kristy, author.
Title: Geographies of journalism : the imaginative power of place
 in making digital news / Robert E Gutsche, Jr. and Kristy Hess.
Description: London ; New York : Routledge, 2019. | Series:
 Disruptions: studies in digital journalism | Includes
 bibliographical references and index.
Identifiers: LCCN 2018022990 | ISBN 9781138554368
 (hardback : alk. paper) | ISBN 9781315148946 (ebook)
Subjects: LCSH: Journalism, Regional. | Digital media—
 Technological innovations. | Online journalism—Social aspects. |
 Place (Philosophy)—Social aspects.
Classification: LCC PN4784.R29 G88 2019 | DDC 070.433—dc23
LC record available at https://lccn.loc.gov/2018022990

ISBN: 978-1-138-55436-8 (hbk)
ISBN: 978-1-315-14894-6 (ebk)

Typeset in Times New Roman
by Apex CoVantage, LLC

Contents

Acknowledgements		vi
Introduction: The power of place-making and journalism		1
1	Mapping the geographies of journalism	7
2	The trichotomy of place, space, and territory in digital journalism studies	21
3	Symbolic and imaginative power: From doxa to innovation in journalism	38
4	Demarcating news space(s) in digital news	52
5	Who is where? Complicating power, proximity, and journalistic authority	67
6	Power, place, and the spatial dialectic of digital journalism	84
	Conclusion: Advancing the research agenda	102
	References	110
	Index	123

Acknowledgements

We are indebted to many academic colleagues for their contributions of knowledge or simply for their inspiration. Together we thank Bob Franklin, who has helped shape a place for us in the wider journalism academy, for his encouragement and support and for building three amazing platforms – *Journalism Studies*, *Journalism Practice*, and *Digital Journalism* – that have become influential places and incubators for journalism scholarship.

I am grateful for a long list of those who support my work, particularly through a challenging year of transitions, including a new baby and a new job. Moving from Miami to Northern England has been a shift in perspectives and environment. I wish to thank my wife, Carolina, for her daily support and love in what has been the production of a work that I have thought about since my doctoral studies. I am also thankful to my parents, Bob and Jeannie, and many others, including Mark Gutsche, Jim Bradford and Liguia Estrada, Mary Fisher, Oscar and Vicky Estrada, Moses Shumow, Juliet Pinto, Maarten Michielse, Manuela Barba, Mathew Wallace, Adan Loughlin, Sam Birkett, Lucy Walton, and Chris Derbyshire. To my coauthor, I am aware of the immense time and energy that she has put into this project, and I am grateful. From special issues to this project and many more to come, I owe you.

–Robert E. (Ted) Gutsche, Jr.

I am grateful to my friends and family who enrich my life on so many levels. To Lisa Waller – our daily catch ups and scholarly adventures add to the sense of place you bring to my life as an academic and a friend. To Julie Rowlands, for sharing her Bourdieusian wisdom, Mum and Dad for instilling the feeling of what it means to "be home," and Angela Morgan for her encouragement. Most importantly, I thank my family – Glen, Alec, Myles, and Ivy – for tolerating the many hours and precious holiday time needed to complete this book. To Ted – I look forward to those rare meetings in person somewhere in the world to keep the ideas flowing. You definitely owe me a drink!

–Kristy Hess

Introduction
The power of place-making and journalism

Our scholarly discussion on the geographies of journalism begins in Hollywood. In 2016, the critically acclaimed film *Lion* premiered and told the true story of a young Indian boy, Saroo Brierley, separated from his family after he fell asleep on a train. The authorities, believing his next of kin to be dead, eventually permitted a well-intended Australian couple to adopt and relocate him to Tasmania. Now living far from his birthplace, Brierley continued to possess the burning desire to find "home." As an adult, he used Google Maps to locate the tiny Indian village where he was raised, drawing on nothing but the childhood memory of a water tower, river, and train line to guide him.

To Google executives, Brierley's story became a triumph of technology. Western media, meanwhile, developed a fascination with the boy actor "plucked from slumdog Mumbai to Hollywood" (Roberts and Sachdeva, 2017) to play the role of Brierley in the film. When the child actor struggled to secure a visa to attend the premiere in the United States, journalists and Hollywood heavyweights were quick to use their influence to rectify the situation (Alexander, 2016). Yet, these same individuals and institutions gave little attention to the fact that hundreds of other Indians were also being denied access to the US amid dramatic changes to border control.

The film – and its subsequent media coverage of technology, trial, and triumph – highlights how economic, cultural, and physical distance from a perceived center are often viewed as obstacles to overcome. Sometimes this "center" is where there is the greatest cluster of resources and power. In other contexts interpretations on geography, people, and related issues may be based on our sense of place in the world – our homes, neighborhoods, or communities.

The production and promotion of *Lion* reveals how media and technology play a role in both bridging and reinforcing these divides and highlights the role – and control – of news media to help connect, shape, and reinforce

2 Introduction

our understandings of places along with the opportunities and inequalities within our geographies.

At its heart, this book unpacks journalism's relationship to geography, especially its relationship to place-making. We are interested in the way news media shape perceptions of location but also how the news shapes people's connection to the physical and digital spaces where journalism is practiced and how this relates to legitimacy and power. By place, we mean the physical, social, and digital spaces and sites to which individuals attribute meaning and which become more significant when this meaning (both imaginative and physical) is shared or contested by others.

Benedict Anderson's (1983) well-cited (yet problematic) notion of imagined communities – despite its top-down and colonial approach to place-making – may indeed highlight the relationship between media and the building of collective identity through a shared sense of time and space. *Geographies of Journalism*, however, questions how this imaginative power works in an increasingly mobile and transient era – from the way we perceive both familiar and unfamiliar places and people to the new territories being carved out by news media in digital landscapes.

Central to this are issues of power and a focus on the role of journalism in patrolling boundaries and generating divides between insiders and outsiders. Social theorists, philosophers, geographers, and communication thinkers from Pierre Bourdieu to David Morley, Doreen Massey and Henri Lefebvre to Edward Soja, bell hooks, and David Harvey inform our thinking throughout this book. The roots of geographic study are combined with concepts of symbolic and imaginative power and violence, ideology, myth and narrative, doxa, ritual, and mobility to consider journalism and its relationship to place.

In unpacking the geographies of journalism, we make an important distinction about the way we understand journalism: there is a need to expand focus from the role of journalism in the public sphere to examine its "place" in the highly contested social sphere. By the social sphere, we mean the realm of our everyday within which our social lives help us make sense of who we are as individuals and ultimately as collectives (Hess and Gutsche, 2018).

It is within these spheres where we construct connections to others beyond our intimate lives and, where appropriate, meaningful behavior and practices are negotiated. News media play a distinct role in establishing social norms which function as forms of social control and order, maintaining approved standards of daily life, institutional structures and practices, and dominant explanations of the world around us.

The social sphere becomes a permeable shell through which journalism scholars can better probe ideas of collectivity, virtue and vice, ritual, myth,

Introduction 3

sociability, social honor, and control as they relate to place. It is our contention that journalists, then, should be examined as active place-makers rather than objective bystanders in the places they serve and that certain media outlets continue to wield more power and influence in certain settings than others. We also strongly believe that journalists should be held accountable to engage with reflexive tools to not only acknowledge this power but to guide journalistic practices into the future.

Too often, scholarship focuses on the "place" of journalism in the digital age through concepts such as boundary work, which is applied similarly in other political and newsroom-centric sociological and cultural studies (Deuze and Witschge, 2017; Wahl-Jorgensen, 2010), to provide an inward-looking view of the norms and conventions shaping the journalistic profession. Such approaches can frequently be at the expense of studying the ways in which news media relate to the spaces and places in which people interact with each other as viewed through a lens of power. In this respect we address power as an ideological process that maintains "winners" and "losers" within society, rooted in language that is aligned with moments of violence (physical and symbolic) that reinforce actions against particular individuals and groups for the benefit of some groups over others.

Throughout the book, and which we unpack later, we discuss the concept of "sense of place." By this concept, we mean a process that generates feelings of inclusion and acceptance but which reminds us that there are always environments where we feel "out of place" – even "put in our place" – and that there are times when these sensibilities are guided by those we deem legitimate place-makers in certain contexts.

Massey's (1991) idea of global sense of place, for instance, points to a "power geometry" in a globalized world. News media and larger media conglomerates continue to be among the power elite which hold influential positions in social flows and movement (Massey, 1994). In the digital realm, for example, filter bubbles can certainly narrow the scope of information flow in online spaces and create a myopic view of the world for a particular user. Yet, we should not overlook the fact that filter bubbles are a new spin on an age-old practice: What makes news and interests us always is determined by our day-to-day practices in the places that "matter," by notions of who we are, where we have been or plan to go, and who we feel belongs alongside us.

More recently, Reese (2017) highlights that a "spatial turn" has made concepts of fields, spheres, and networks much more relevant in the digital age while assemblages and nodes have become increasingly part of the conversation of mapping journalism's new virtual terrain. In this book, however, we begin by returning to the roots of geography studies – especially

4 *Introduction*

its physical, social, and cultural dimensions – to provide a foundation for understanding journalists as place-makers in the digital era.

This book provides an overview of geography as an area of study and outlines foundational areas and debates relevant to journalism over time – physical, social, cultural, media, and the material turns. This means traversing and condensing wide scholarly terrain; however, it is not our intention to provide an encyclopedia of geography studies here. What we have sought to do is highlight the gaps in and the richness of this field to create a kaleidoscope of complementary lenses through which to approach geography and journalism.

Throughout each chapter, we draw on news media coverage and interviews with practicing journalists to illustrate key contentions. This involves data from qualitative studies undertaken as part of our own research as individuals during the past several years that canvasses parts of Australia and the United States. Our specific research focus has been across the local media sector, which offers a particularly rich area of inquiry for a book about place-making given we can study journalism's intricate relationship to place in smaller settings, whilst acknowledging its role in wider global flows and movements (Gutsche, 2014a; Hess, 2013).

At times we adopt a pooled case comparison approach (see Oldfather and West, 1995). Pooled research is a form of secondary data analysis that has emerged in more post-modern qualitative studies. The approach makes use of pre-existing raw research data (interviews, diary entries, and focus group transcripts) for the purpose of investigating new questions or verifying previous studies (Heaton, 2004). Oldfather and West (1995) argue that "pooled case comparison" is based on the informal sharing of qualitative data.

In contrast with comparative methods that begin with interpreted findings, pooled case comparison sets aside categories and properties from previous analyses (Oldfather and West, 1995). Raw data from separate studies are literally pooled to create a new data set from which fresh categories and properties are derived and the sources of individual bits of data remain visible throughout the analysis.

Overview of the book

Chapter 1 provides the overview of geography studies in Western contexts during the past several decades. This return to the roots of geographic underpinnings provides a much-needed foundational landscape upon which to build this and other projects that use terms such as "space" and "place" interchangeably or lack a historical context in how geography can be viewed from physical, social, cultural, economic, digital, and media perspectives.

Introduction 5

These approaches are applied throughout the book to push boundaries of how current work within the field of journalism studies addresses geographic elements.

A book on geography would be insufficient without a discussion on the key debates around place and space and their relationship to news media and journalism. This book situates issues of power at the forefront of such discussions, as presented in Chapter 2, to highlight the power of territory as a vital yet often overlooked component of the space and place literature in relation to journalism. The trichotomy of place, space, and territory prompts a recalibration between the need for speed and mobility and the careful construction of space and place over time. Through this discussion, the relationship between news media and Facebook and the contestation for political, moral, and social influence is highlighted. It is here we argue that the social sphere is the new highly contested territory that warrants a much greater emphasis in discussions on journalism's relationship to place and space.

In Chapter 3, we explore the symbolic and "imaginative power of place." Here, we adopt and merge theories of social space and cultural meaning to equip the professional journalist (and scholars) with the reflexive tools to understand the power of and the power inherent within place-making. We draw on Bourdieu's notion of symbolic power – the power to construct reality – as a precondition for imaginative power – that is the power to imagine or construct what we cannot see or to reinforce meanings of reality through verisimilitude. Complementary constructs of myth and doxa are also adopted to demonstrate how certain dominant ideas are reinforced and perpetuated by those with symbolic power, including journalists.

We highlight the notion of "imaginative power," meanwhile, as that which enables place-makers to be innovative, creative, and to envisage or discover the news all the while building upon the dominant and frequently hegemonic presuppositions of the creator and audience related to location and populations. Indeed, imaginative power should not be considered emancipatory, as it can be used to generate binaries – ideals and fallacies – especially in terms of what we cannot see or those who are in places at a distance from our own.

In Chapter 4, we outline the demarcation of space and news zones. This may seem like we are covering old ground, but the ways in which spaces and places are constructed have received little attention in journalism studies and so it is important that we build this foundation here. In this chapter, we argue more work is needed to understand the way journalists demarcate the physical boundaries in which they generate news before territories evolve and before rules and ritualistic practices are cemented. We pay specific attention to news media and the demarcation of space in physical geography, that is the neighborhoods, suburbs, towns, and cities where we

6   *Introduction*

live, work, and play as a sometimes forgotten or understated starting point in complicating news in digital spheres. We then discuss the characterization of these zones in the context of cultural geography and the relationship to the symbolic and imaginary power of place.

Chapter 5 sees us extend our thinking around other important concepts such as proximity and distance in the context of place-making given their integral relationship to news values and journalism. We contend that existing scholarship on news proximity tends to bypass one of the most important dimensions of them all – proximity to power (both physical and imagined) in changing physical and digital contexts.

Here, we pay particular attention to what we term "performative proximity," which reinforces media power in places of meaning in the digital age. By performative proximity we mean the coming together of powerful elites in physical and digital and virtual space to not only reinforce the significance of an event or issue but to reinforce the legitimacy of those who are "there" – and, in effect, those who are not. In discussing proximity, we also extend upon three other elements – socio-ideological proximity, temporal proximity, and the way audiences perceive journalistic proximity to places.

Chapter 6 shifts to a critical examination of news media and their relationship to social surveillance and control in the spaces and places they serve. We highlight political developments using technology to control, but also focus on the cultural dimensions of shaming and boundary work to shape acceptable behavior and expectations within places. In so doing, this chapter further aligns geographies of journalism with the social justice and critical geographic studies of those who examine elements of the "right to the city" that place people and collectives at the center of public place-making.

The book concludes with a discussion of the challenges ahead for journalists as place-makers in a period of rapid mobility and change. It highlights several suggested methodological approaches (arguably underdeveloped in journalism studies) to examine the geographies of journalism from anthropology that crosses physical and digital terrain to affective and critical cartography, critical and reflexive studies, and border studies.

1 Mapping the geographies of journalism

Geography has a rich and long history of academic inquiry. It is no wonder ideas about locale and terrain feature in just about every scholarly discipline in some shape or form given that no matter what we do in any moment we are always situated "somewhere." Like our DNA, every place on Earth and in digital space is different – from unique geographical to digital URL coordinates to shape, form, function, and meaning. A one-size-fits-all approach to understanding journalism and place-making just doesn't work. Context is king.

Journalist Nick Davies (2009) coined the term "Flat Earth News" to argue that the truth of journalism was about as false as the idea that the Earth is flat. It is perhaps ironic then that journalism scholars have been accused of propagating a "Flat Earth" view of geography studies for decades by offering a two-dimensional approach to debates about space and place, using geography as a descriptor of location or "a GPS perspective that can easily miss the inherent sociality that produces it" (Peters, 2015, p. 3).[1]

There have, of course, been attempts to build physical geography into more three-dimensional accounts of news and its relationship to wider global information flows and movements. This involves concepts of geo-social journalism (Hess and Waller, 2017), locative journalism (Nyre, Bjørnestad, and Øie, 2012), locative news (Goggin, Martin, and Dwyer, 2015), and place-based knowledge and spatial journalism (Schmitz Weiss, 2015). Geo-social journalism, for example, has been used to understand local media, situating:

> news outlets' solid link to territory, while acknowledging the wider social space in which it plays a role – both in holding an influential position in certain social flows and movements and as a node to wider global news media and communications networks.
>
> (Hess, 2013, p. 45)

8 *Mapping the geographies of journalism*

In recent work on digital journalism, however, those whom have cited such scholarship tend to overemphasis the digital component and downplay the geographic. While geo-social is a concept generated by one of us here to fuse the physical, social, and digital realms, there is still much to be done in laying the geographic groundwork. It is our aim to excavate and reveal the three-dimensionality of geography as it relates to journalism studies in the hope it can take its rightful place, front and center in debates about the future of news.

Geography can, of course, be taken quite literally to refer to the physical features of the Earth and its atmosphere, and we do not intend to discount the significance of this here. Geography also relates, however, to human activity and how the former shapes and is shaped by social and cultural influences (Petersen, Sack, and Gabler, 2017). Important to this discussion, geography, as a term, implies that the world operates spatially and temporally and that social relations do not operate independently of place and environment but are thoroughly grounded in and through them.

What often distinguishes geography and human geography from other disciplines is the application of a set of core geographical concepts to the phenomena under investigation, including space, place, territory, and mobility. Critical and cultural geography – a sub-discipline of human geography – has arguably been the most influential dimension of geography studies when it comes to media studies more broadly, as the emphasis is on the representation of places and the power dynamics that shape influential meaning makers in society (Hall, 1980; Monmonier, 1997; Williams, 1983).

This movement overall has, however, been at the expense of other important dimensions of geography, especially in terms of the physical, social, and more recently material and digital geographies, which when fused together, ground our understanding of "geography" as it relates to journalism.

Physical geography: Meaning-making with our feet on the ground

We begin this section by returning to the disciplinary origins of geographic study – physical geography and the connection to Earth. This may appear awkward, dare we suggest backward, in a book about news in the digital era. What continually surprises us, however, is the increasing emphasis on digital tools and networks at the expense of a "feet on the ground" approach to the study of journalism as it relates to space and place.

Physical geography concentrates on spatial and environmental processes that shape the natural world. It considers aspects of spatial patterns of weather, climate, soils, vegetation, animals, and landforms and generates

Mapping the geographies of journalism 9

well-defined areas of study from oceanography and cartography to astronomy and meteorology.

In journalism studies, some scholars suggest that because we can now access news anywhere and everywhere, the significance of these elements and descriptions of physical geography are redundant (Meyrowitz, 1985; Sparks, 2000) – an especially prominent prediction among those who began contemplating the effects of the internet and technology long before the rise of the iPhone and Facebook.

Meyrowitz (1985) most notably suggested electronic media alters our "situational geography" by undermining "the traditional relationship between physical setting and social situation" (pp. 6–7), while futurist Thornton May told *The Wall Street Journal* in 1998 that communications technology had become so powerful that he predicted "by the year 2008, technology will have trivialized the concept of 'place'" and, to put his point simply, that "Geography . . . is dead" (Bulkeley, 1998).

Giving the physical environment credence in the geographies of journalism does not mean we resort to a type of environmental determinism. There is scope to consider the value of place-based knowledge to the way the natural environment shapes journalistic practices and policies – even in a digital context. For example, our own studies highlight how the distinctive "natural" elements of the environments in which we live shape everyday cultural and ritualistic practices but also that the types of stories journalists produce about everyday life depend upon their interpretations of their physical location – from stories about rising sea levels in Miami (Shumow and Gutsche, 2016) to agriculture in regional Australia (Hess, 2013).

Physical geography also certainly provides a scholarly mantle for those studying environmental journalism. Here, scholarship seeks to balance the scientific and physical dimensions of geography with cultural meaning (Bødker and Neverla, 2012).

It is also perhaps taken for granted that the unevenness of the Earth's natural features can play a role in generating inequalities when it comes to our level of access to telecommunications services. Information and communication "blackspots" – poor internet and phone coverage within certain geographic terrain – for example, hills and valleys – is a real and expensive issue for some governments and telecommunication companies, playing a part in generating an increasingly digital divide, especially among rural and regional media users (see Freeman and Park, 2017).[2]

Poor quality or no access to broadband services limits the digital innovation of local newspapers, which continue to depend on the print product for reliability and accessibility – as well as the functionality of journalism to serve broad populations. Bushfires which tore through several

10   *Mapping the geographies of journalism*

Victorian and New South Wales communities in Australia in March 2018, for instance, highlight the informational inequalities generated by geographic distance from metropolitan centers and challenges presented by the natural topography.

During that crisis, the Australian Broadcasting Corporation (ABC) reported that mobile phone and internet blackspots were putting rural lives at risk as many people had been unable to access information online or via phone to receive alerts (Neal, Miles, and Martin, 2018). One local member of Parliament said the natural topography of the area was contributing to the issue of poor phone coverage while others highlighted the geographic distance from centers of power, a representation perhaps, of the lasting inequality maintained by the inaction of elected governance.

One resident was quoted as saying by the ABC, "For far too long, this town has been forgotten with mobile telecommunications because we aren't in Sydney." Yet another reader commented on the ABC's Facebook page to identify similar forms of inequality based on intersections of geography, distance, and imaginations of the population far from the center of power:

> Guess what people, living in country Victoria means you get to pay all the rates and taxes that everyone else does, but when it comes to services and infrastructure;. what? Who the hell are you? And why should we care? I live in country Victoria so I know.
> (ABC, South-west Victoria Facebook page, 2018)

In subsequent chapters, we examine the rural/metropolitan or city/country divide as an under-examined yet specific aspect of the interplay between journalism and geography. Below, we move to another sphere of understanding central to our interpretation of geographies of journalism – the role of sociability.

Social geography and the social meanings of journalism

We are by nature social beings, and so the way we gather and interact *within* physical and digital environments is a key component of geography studies. Yet in journalism studies, dominant understandings of the social are shifting into dangerous territory (Hess and Gutsche, 2018). Increasingly, the idea of the social is considered synonymous with social media and social networking in which the public writ large is engaged (or is invited to engage) in a mediated sphere of public meaning (Dutton and Dubois, 2015).

Terms such as social journalism, social news, and the sociability of news have been coined to explore how social networking is shaping journalism,

Mapping the geographies of journalism 11

from its celebrated Fifth Estate function to audience and journalistic engagement and participation and perceptions of digital platforms. Phillips (2012), for example, positions "sociability" in journalism as news produced in a form that is capable of spreading virally (p. 669).

What is often overlooked in studies that examine the relationship between journalism and social media is the very significance of our connection to "place" – the imagined meanings of physical locations – that drives demand for these new platforms and for understanding journalism. Equating the "social" as a descriptor of digital networks and technological tools tends to bury the importance of social theory and the rich theoretical and philosophical insights it brings to journalism.

It is not just the rise of social media tools, however, that has detracted scholarly attention from the importance of social geography to journalism practice and scholarship. Despite being one of the oldest forms of human geography, social geography has for the past several decades been overshadowed by a cultural turn within geography studies itself – so much so that the lines between the two are often unclear (Cresswell, 2010).

Whereas cultural geography has come to focus more on meaning-making within and about places, at its heart social geography explores the interactions of spatial structure and social structure and the issues of marginalization, classifications, and power they present within spaces and related meanings.[3]

The early relationship between social geography and journalism is most evident in urban studies, where the city and neighborhood became a contextually specific site of influence to examine social structures, as well as racial and class integration. The controversial work of Robert Park (1922), among others, highlighted the role of ethnic print newspapers in bringing minority groups together in a particular geographic place.

To be clear, however, as with much early social science approaches to race and geography – as well as the form and purpose of communication – these initial glances are rooted in historical positions of racial stratification. Park also clearly differentiated his human ecology approach from geography, preferring to focus on the interactions between individuals. But he did position the notion of community as synonymous with physical places (Park, 1926).

It was this particular emphasis that strongly influenced studies of local news media for much of the 20th Century, especially in regards to the local press and its relationship to community-building and social capital – what political scientist Robert Putnam (2000) theorized as the collective "glue" binding societies together (see also, Richards, 2013). Here, it has been suggested that small towns and cities located at a distance from a perceived

12 *Mapping the geographies of journalism*

metropolitan center are more likely to generate social capital and engage with news.

In this book, again, we are concerned that critical tenets of social geography have at times been lost in research about journalism and social order (Hess and Gutsche, 2018). Issues of marginalization of geography as a complicating (and complicated) element of journalism and communication have instead been largely subsumed by cultural studies.[4] For us here, then, it is social geography's commitment to the structures, processes, and labels that shape the spatial organization (and integration) of people that is important to retain in the geographies of journalism (for more on critical elements of geographic studies, see Cresswell [2010]).

Links to social geography, too, enable a political economy dimension to journalism and place, providing scope to capture the role of the journalistic field and its associated norms and values in constructing the types of news that matters in geographic and digital places – even the failure to position place-making as a key convention shaping journalism practice. From this perspective we can engage with how news media use technology and journalism practices to connect people with each other in places.

Social geography can, too, emphasize a "place-matters" approach to the government policies and economic restraints of media that shape the often-invisible boundaries of "where" certain news media can be broadcast or published. Examples of these manifestations of invisible boundaries include broadcast licensing agreements, the issue of media streaming, foreign media ownership, and high-speed broadband coverage.

Of course, it is certainly cultural geography where the meaning-making function of locations – or imaginations of locations (i.e., notions of "The Middle East" or a neighboring, unfamiliar city) – is perhaps best explored, providing it is considered alongside the questions other tenets of geography might present. Cultural geography, for example, gives agency to both the power elite and the practices of everyday people in the shaping of news as a place of its own and is central to understanding journalism as place-makers in the digital age.

Cultural geography: Where control and communication collide

As we have ascertained, social geography has laid claim to addressing issues of marginalization and inequalities, but it is the influence of cultural geography that has received the most recent attention in this space among media and communication scholars (Ali, 2016; Gutsche, 2014a). It is through a cultural approach that we appreciate the power of news media to shape the way we give meaning to places.

Mapping the geographies of journalism   13

And while it is not a great revelation to suggest that journalists help to connect and construct understandings of the world, cultural studies more broadly reminds us that language is not a transparent form of communication somehow simply describing what is "there" (Cosgrove and Daniels, 1988; Zonn, 1990).

A key focus here is understanding how we carve out spaces of identity and meaning via media in a transient, mobile world and how journalism seems to define our experiences of being "on the scene" of some news event. In digital spaces, for example, place-making becomes a deeper imaginative function reliant on subjectivities of use and not lived experience.

The changing nature of the cultural "landscape"

As a field of study, cultural geography has splintered into several directions, but its foundations have been largely attributed to classical landscape studies, notably the work of Carl Sauer (1925) who shifted from geography's positivist ontology toward more humanistic understandings of our impact on the natural world. We highlight the significance of landscape studies here, considering its continued synergies to journalism practice, which we shall discuss shortly.

Classical landscape studies offered a largely two-dimensional foray into cultural geography. Sauer, for example, considered human impacts on the natural landscape and environment to be a manifestation of culture – focusing on cultural artifacts rather than the processes and practices that generated them. A more sophisticated approach emerged from the 1960s (Cosgrove and Jackson, 1987) which signaled two important shifts, including (1) a broader interpretation of "landscape" as something more fluid and not fixed to the natural environment such as non-material dimensions of space and place, or the study of objects and texts as landscapes in their own right and (2) an emphasis on cultural politics, with the latter placing heavy emphasis on the politics of representation and issues of power and resistance.

This latter approach shared synergies with studies on intersections of ideology and verisimilitude that transfix political boundaries and borders to meanings of nationalism and orientalism (Bhabha, 1990; Said, 1979). Raymond Williams (1976) contributed interpretations of "city" and "country" via gendered meanings (the city being masculine and focused on industrialization, the country feminine in its creation of sustenance and maintenance of tradition). This approach situates the divide between rural and metropolitan journalism which evolved in scholarship during the mid-20th Century.

In adopting a critical lens, we also see the continuation of the significance of "landscape" through the work of scholars such as David Morley (2000),

14   *Mapping the geographies of journalism*

who has focused on media technologies in constituting "electronic land-scapes" within which we live. For Morley, the emphasis is on those who are considered to have a "place" in certain landscapes and those who don't, which is instrumental to the critical approach we take here. Morley (2000) highlights the rise of closed communities online built on a culture of fear of the unknown and the unfamiliar. Morley (2006) also contends that geography is a process of mobility, identity, and territoriality, and in digital space we see some of the oldest and regressive structures of exclusion occur.

What makes a "good" or "inviting" city or digital space for one group of people can in turn make that same city alienating or dangerous for another. Often, mythical archetypes of good and evil, of monsters and heroes, are deployed in news coverage to establish these binaries. There too has been little attention paid within a cultural geography framework to the performances, practices, and rituals established (both consciously and unconsciously) by journalists and audiences that reinforce people's connection to the places they live or travel through, both in physical and digital realms.[5]

Nor has there been extensive discussion on the way material objects transform into "places of meaning" for people who consume the news. We will discuss media and ritual in Chapter 3, but it is important to note that people make choices concerning how to "perform" their identities depending not only on *who* they are with but *where* they are, though the consequences of interpretation, behavior, and expression relate to a given space and a place (Goffman, 1959; Latham, 2008; Turner, 1988).

Cultural geography provides scope to consider both the performances and practices that evolve within places, emphasizing the shift beyond issues of representation towards understanding how everyday people engage with news through constructions of identity and power. In this way, people's identities tied to place are produced through ongoing and active relationships to other people and places via experience, rituals, storytellings of experience, and imagination.

Media and the material turn in cultural geography

The "new" cultural geography turn from the 1960s generated intense discussion around the very nature and fluidity of space and place (see Chapter 2). Media geography – which emerged as an offshoot in the 1980s (Burgess and Gold, 1985) – has canvassed everything from comics and film to dance and cartography, even how postal services consider the representation of places in their work (Adams, Craine, and Dittmer, 2014). Media geography has, for example, raised questions about how dominant ideologies are

Mapping the geographies of journalism   15

imposed by the media versus the degree to which audiences actively shape the meaning of media products.

Craine (2016) argues that media geography explores broad questions of material production, cultural meaning, and bodily affects in relation to the practices and processes by which geographical information is gathered, geographical facts are ordered, and imaginative geographies are created. Within media geography, there are few specific studies that explore in detail the relationship between journalism and place-making.

Paul Adams (2018) has most recently called on journalism scholars to consider the visual elements of overt place-making within journalism. He performs a critical analysis of how journalists visualize "communities," nations, borders, and boundaries, in news articles on refugees, asylum seekers, and immigrants entering Europe, for instance, with eye-catching maps featuring brightly colored arrows converging on Europe from various directions, scaled to represent aggregated human flows. Adams, therefore, highlights how news maps reflect choices on what to include and exclude and promote biases that influence dangerous social policies and act against populations and individuals (see also, Gutsche, 2014a; Salovaara, 2016).

Digital journalism and its place within functions of the internet, mobility, and innovative storytelling and information-gathering have redefined physical "location" as a keyword in search engine inquiries. An emphasis on big and open data sources and methods that support spatial planning and decision making have also emerged as means by which to shape understandings of the world that appear as maps or as "evidence-based" explanations for social conditions, demographics, and trends.

Amidst these twists and turns of geographic study as it relates to media and the digital, there remains scope to carve out a new and specific focus on journalism. There has been increasing concern that the pendulum has swung too far within the tenet of cultural geography into the rudderless domain of space and place and that there is a need to reassert the importance of the material world more broadly. The rise of digital space has prompted, for example, a resurging interest in journalism studies toward the material – especially through technological innovation and digitized objects and tools (see Anderson and Maeyer, 2014).

In journalism studies, scholars celebrate the rise of geo-spatial tools to algorithms and most recently "immersive journalism" via augmented and virtual reality (Jones, 2017). Yet, quite often the theoretical lenses for examining journalism and materiality are drawn from science and philosophy traditions (rather than geography or cultural studies) with Latour (2005) and Deleuze and Guattarri (1988) as particular favorites when considering

16   *Mapping the geographies of journalism*

the interplay between man, machine, and non-human networks as agents of change in journalism practice.

Primo and Zago (2015), for example, use Latour's actor network theory to argue that besides asking who "does journalism" in the digital age it is necessary to assess "what does" journalism and how technological actants transform journalism practices. At first glance, assemblage and network theories appear most useful because they help us grasp the variety of ways in which journalism practices are interwoven with media technology. Social networking theories, especially when integrated into Geographical Information System (GIS) settings, for example, can help to model how humans socialize, share information, and form social groups within a complex geographic landscape.

But there are weaknesses we cannot overlook here in a book focused on place-making, including the roles of critical interactions with technology and power (Couldry and Hepp, 2017).

Of course, we do acknowledge that not all relationships are always hierarchical – they can intersect and traverse, potentially perpetuating the status quo while also offering new ways to contest it (Arnould and Thompson, 2015). We argue, however, that in discussions of journalism and place-making there must always be room to distinguish between human and non-human actors. Dare we say, the re-emphasis on scholarship into the non-human dimensions of geography has perhaps not swung back far enough.

As we foregrounded earlier, we must return to the roots of geography and include the natural world as it impacts on journalism practice. As much as the iPhone has become a "living" landscape in itself, we must not overlook the Earth, its climates and terrain which play a role in shaping our news media-related practices that connect us to places. Indeed, journalism is inevitably imbricated in a web of human and non-human relations, but in considering technological innovation we must always keep our feet firmly planted on the ground.

Bringing it all together: The perfect storm of weather coverage

To bring the physical, social, cultural, and digital dimensions of the geographies of journalism together there is perhaps no better illustration than news media and its relationship to the weather. While there are studies that examine the role of journalism in the reporting of natural disasters and crisis, there has been little attention paid to the very significance of the weather and climate to journalism practice, our sense of place, and the "news" (Henson, 2010).

Mapping the geographies of journalism   17

What once was a broadcast ritual – we would learn of tomorrow's weather nightly at the end of a television news bulletin or radio broadcast – we now have a constant commitment to meteorology by-the-minute, accessible from our tablets and devises, pushed to us via alerts or with the click of a button.

The importance of the weather to our daily lives goes to the heart of social order and appeals to our sense of place in the world. Smartphones give us the choice of tapping into the places that matter to us as individuals – towns and cities where we live, have visited on holidays, or where we have family, friends, or work connections. In the US, The Weather Channel serves as a 24-hour weather news channel, and expert "weather" coverage continues to be a main branding mechanism for local television news (Daniels and Loggins, 2010).

Indeed, media scholars have highlighted that via traditional broadcast mediums, the weather itself can be nationalized and its national limits clearly demarcated in the average weather forecast (Monmonier, 1997). Wild weather reported "elsewhere" creates the idea of safety at "home" and speaks to the continued popularity of news coverage about conditions beyond our borders that might not be easily signposted via our mobile devices (Papastergiadis, 1998; Scannell, 1996). Morley (2006) highlights research, for example, on the importance of the weather among members of Slovenian-speaking minority groups in Austria who make a point of tuning into the weather forecast on the radio, because they feel that it helps keeps them in connection to both sides of the border.

Of course, as we highlighted earlier, there is perhaps no news event that more powerfully illustrates the interplay of the geographies of journalism than natural disasters – especially cyclones, floods, fires, storms, and tsunamis. From a social geography perspective, journalists continue to serve a legitimate, reliable connector role, advising audiences within places where to go and what to do when crisis hits – often with the support of geo-spatial technology.

The battle to be perceived as the "go-to" site for information in times of need should not be underestimated in the digital environment, yet increasingly news outlets have directed this traffic to their news outlets' Facebook pages rather than developing their own nodes of power in digital space for such purposes. From a sociological perspective, too, McLemore (2016) highlights the various news values and journalistic norms behind the scenes that influenced coverage of major flooding in Arkansas in the US, which killed 13 people in 2016. McLemore contends locals accused big media outlets of ignoring the story which he suggests was due to several factors, especially the timing of the event. Here, the storm hit at a challenging moment of the media calendar during summer vacation in August, when news resources were tied up with Olympic Games and ongoing presidential elections.

18 *Mapping the geographies of journalism*

Meanings associated with the flooding were left largely out of the national media, McLemore argues, because "it was just the wrong kind of suffering" in that it dealt with cultures and classes of the US that rarely made big news and that held little social capital. McLemore also deals with "location" by highlighting the importance of physical geography in a digital world. In this case, the rural areas most affected were difficult to locate and to "get to" given the terrain.

The meaning-making role of journalism akin to cultural geography, meanwhile, truly kicks in after the weather settles when journalists continue to draw on mythical archetypes and narratives of the hero's journey and overcoming challenges to create a sense of collective memory and identity for audiences located within place (Fry, 2003; Gutsche and Salkin, 2013; Lule, 2001).

Those without a connection to the places where dramatic weather events occur, meanwhile, often learn about such disasters via news outlets, and they, too, become familiar with imaginations of geography. To begin that conversation in place-making, here, however, consider the following: While Facebook's Mark Zuckerberg may have developed an interface for global social connection, his venture into virtual reality attracted criticism when he failed to appreciate the value of cultural narrative and context in a promotional video for his VR platform, Spaces.

Zuckerberg came under fire for posting a "tasteless" video that showed him touring flooded Puerto Rican streets in virtual reality in the wake of Hurricane Maria in 2017 (McGoogan, 2017). The video shows Zuckerberg's avatar highlighting the features of his VR platform against the backdrop of the devastation. "One of the things that's really magical about virtual reality," he says, "is you can get the feeling that you're really in a place."

After many people criticized the VR broadcast in the comments on his Facebook profile, Zuckerberg apologized:

> One of the most powerful features of VR is empathy. My goal here was to show how VR can raise awareness and help us see what's happening in different parts of the world. Reading some of the comments, I realize this wasn't clear, and I'm sorry to anyone this offended.
>
> (Solon, 2017)

What we argue here is that Zuckerberg's VR experience highlights that despite our increasing technological capabilities, the power of place-making is real and intensifying. A failure to acknowledge this can affect the legitimacy and credibility of the information provider.

Mapping the geographies of journalism 19

Conclusion: Geographic shifts, journalistic steps

The shifting nature of geography studies over time has been much like a slow-moving hovercraft. It began with its engines firmly on the ground with an approach that encouraged us to be deeply in-tune with our relationship to the natural landscape, before social and cultural studies moved the joy stick upwards, hovering above the Earth to engage in much more abstract discussions of space and place, of interconnecting constellations, social forces, and issues of representation and social and cultural meaning.

Whilst the rise of digital technology has exacerbated this, it too has led to renewed emphasis on the material dimensions of space and place. Metaphorically speaking, the aircraft control pad has become an actor alongside the pilot in propelling the hovercraft forward. It is our intention to acknowledge these major developments in geographic study, whilst steering the hovercraft back down to solid ground, all the while appreciating the many g-forces that have come to shape this area of study.

The aim of this chapter has been to reveal the three-dimensional layers of geography studies and its relevance to journalism. This is incomplete, however, without a more nuanced discussion about the relationship between place-making and power. In the next chapter we outline the trichotomy of place, space, and territory as it relates to journalism, drawing much more deeply on the relationship between news media and "new" conglomerates such as Facebook and Google. This discussion paves the way for us to consider useful thinking tools of symbolic and imaginative power that explain how journalists both reinforce dominant ideologies about places yet wield imaginative power to shape what we cannot see that can have both positive and ramifications for people and places see it, or who cannot see it.

Notes

1 Cresswell (1996), too, argues that geography should be read "in addition to, rather than instead of, interaction between social groups" (p. 11).
2 To be clear, the digital divide extends beyond terrain and includes intentional creation of spaces under governmental or military and police rule in which internet access is against the wishes of the power elite or in areas or individual spaces of limited economic conditions where "smart phones" and internet connection are not possible.
3 For example, 19th-Century scholar Elisse Reclus – credited with early social geographic thought – set out to explain the spatial inequalities in and of societies and intervene in its organization (see Casino, 2009). In this way, social geography was a deeply political act, yet while political geography focused on geopolitics and empire, social geography emerged with a focus on much more localized political questions that revolved around natural environments. In the 1920s, however, the sharp political orientation of social geography became blunted in favor of a more

20 *Mapping the geographies of journalism*

objective, scientific orientation of sociology with national census data used to gain insight into people's relationships and social positions in place.

4 The difference between the social and cultural geography is perhaps best exemplified in the field of anthropology, where, for example, cultural studies attempts to understand culture as the major way in which human beings adapt to their environment by examining both texts of representation and human behavior that is learned, shared, and typical of a particular group. Social anthropology, on the other hand, concentrates on social relations such as family, kinship, political organization, economic organization religion, law, and social control (Dash, 2004).

5 Scholarly interpretations of geographies are frequently highly contested by those living, experiencing, and even imagining them. How we view location and sense of being in a given space operates in both local and global contexts, as well as personal spaces in which we position our own selves within the dominant meanings of location. This resonates, for example, with studies that explore the relationship between media and diaspora cultures and their relationship to places via media and the news – how people and collectives come to feel both "in" and "out of place" at any given moment (see Langellier, 2010).

2 The trichotomy of place, space, and territory in digital journalism studies

Research highlighting the affects that tablets have on our physical health has made global headlines in recent years (Hodgekiss, 2015; Kreglow, 2015). The term "iPad neck" has been coined in news media reports to highlight the intense strain on our muscles and spine from over-using such devices, and a Japanese company has started cashing in on our changing media practices by selling thumb extensions to help people with small hands navigate smart phones (O'Callaghan, 2014).

Amused parents have even uploaded YouTube footage of toddlers attempting to change channels on the television by swiping their hands across the screen rather than use a remote control. Australian business journalist Nick Vega (2017), in complaining about "texting thumb" – what he describes as pain in the first digit from too much device time – reflected to readers the following:

> Here's some of the things I use my phone for each day:
>
> - Alarm clock
> - Texting my friends
> - Scanning social media
> - Reading the news
> - Listening to music and podcasts
> - Checking sports scores
> - Taking pictures
> - Scheduling appointments
> - Managing my finances
>
> . . . From the moment I wake up until I'm getting ready for bed, my iPhone is constantly in my hand.

There is no doubt the use of digital media tools has become an everyday practice for many of us. Such devices are now, in Martin Heidegger's (1927)

22 *The trichotomy in digital journalism studies*

terms, "ready-to-hand" (p. 415), yet this chapter stops short of adopting a technological determinist approach to examining news media and journalism in the digital age which is often celebratory in tone. Rather, our following words offer a provocation to it.

Vega, in lamenting the rise of texting thumb above, highlights with banal accuracy the various social, cultural, and economic aspects of our world that are increasingly being funneled through – not necessarily determined by – digital tools and software interfaces. At times, however, journalism scholars can focus too intently on the technological implications for reporting the news in places or how people consume it instead of considering the much richer social and cultural conditions that drive and shape the very need for information about people and places.

In this chapter, we pay particular attention to synthesizing and extending the literature on place and space to consider why and how we engage or are subtly coerced into certain spaces and sites of media competition. Peters (2015) argues that applying the spatial turn to thinking about contemporary news consumption means not only thinking about the different ways that far-off places have become closer, but also about the materiality, meaning, and practices of situated moments of "news" use. While there is certainly scope to consider the agency of technology and its influence on journalism practices, we add a missing piece of the theoretical jigsaw in the journalism literature on space and place to date – that of media territory.

Territory: A missing element in journalism studies

It is well established in scholarly literature that spaces become places when bestowed with meaning or significance by those who engage with them. For news media to dominate or hold power in places, then, we must examine space, place and "territory" as a necessary trichotomy (Duarte, 2017). There, are constant symbolic battle lines being drawn by news outlets over their perceived legitimacy to serve, define, patrol, defend, or protect their own interests in a defined space. It is surprising that this argument about the role of territory in these processes has not been as clearly positioned before in the literature on digital journalism, especially given that attempts to carve out media territories in online spaces are occurring at a rapid pace.

The connection between media and territory has a rich scholarly underpinning – from ideas of nationalism to our "sense of community" that play out across macro and micro levels of society, which we will discuss in the next chapter.

In fact, it is well-documented that news media, too, can be used as a tool of influence within the political field to relay propaganda in order to reinforce or assert territorial boundaries (Nohrstedt, Kaitatzi-Whitlock, Ottosen,

The trichotomy in digital journalism studies 23

and Riegert, 2000). At times, there can even be tensions between the state and news media in patrolling and defining cultural boundaries within and across geographic territories, especially during moments of crisis such as terrorism or political events like Brexit (Bødker and Ngomba, 2018; Gutsche and Hess, 2018).

In our definition, news media territories emerge when there is a taken-for-granted assumption that certain media objects, sites, and brands represent collective ideas or values and enact rules, norms, and ritualistic behavior in support of those identities. For news media territories to exist, however, people must believe – albeit subconsciously – that certain media agents have the power to indeed lay claim to such places and spaces. A digital WordPress site set up by a student blogger is not a territory until it can meet these expectations. It may have cultural meaning to some, but not one of wide, collectively acknowledged power. Consequently, we must not see territory as natural, but cultural – a social product linked to desire, power, and identity (Lemos, 2010).

Below, we outline the interdependence between place and news media territory. We continue to draw on exemplars from our own research into local media and critically engage with the über-territorial battle between news media and social media juggernaut Facebook over news territory to highlight our key contentions.

Building to territory: Spaces and places of journalism

Since McLuhan's (2001) global village and Baudrillard's (1983) contention that "henceforth it is the map that precedes the territory" (p. 2), much academic attention has focused on the order of movement and communication across flows and spaces (Castells, 2010) or "time-space compression" (Harvey, 1989). Simply put, such scholarship highlights how technologies from transport to email, internet, and media broadcasting have created a geographical stretching of social relations (Massey, 1994).

Lash and Urry (1994), for example, argue "that the paradigmatic modern experience is that of rapid mobility across often long distances" (p. 253), a shift Bauman (1998) suggests can emancipate people from territorial constraints, allowing them unprecedented freedom to move and act at a distance (p. 159). Shortly, we shall engage more deeply with the literature on territory, but it is important to note that when it comes to space and place, journalism scholars have tended to hone in on issues of convenience, mobility, and speed (Westlund, 2013) and how these factors shape news production and consumption, especially in a digital environment.[1]

Peters (2015) highlights how journalism in the 21st Century is now produced to facilitate mobile places of consumption at a faster pace and

24 *The trichotomy in digital journalism studies*

to provide multiple channels of access for audiences. In engaging with the literature on space and place, then, we encourage a much slower pace when it comes to exploring the temporal dimensions of not only journalism practice itself but people's media-related practices. That is, we call for the need to appreciate the time required to foster an understanding of people's connection to and their evolving "sense of" place in new mediated spaces.

Space

A wide range of scholars – including philosophers, physicists, geographers, architects, and sociologists – have for centuries discussed the importance of space in human existence, yet there is still no clear, consensual definition. Space is perhaps best positioned as something formed by and which mediates our relations with other beings, entities, and flows.

Influential media scholar Manuel Castells (2010), in his conceptualized "network society," suggests space is society. For Castells, modern cities are constructed around a "space of flows" where geographic locations can be seen to be part of a local-global network defined by important information and interaction. Castells considers "space of flows" a spatial logic that determines the expressions of society and is associated with functionality, power, politics, and wealth.

A limitation to the space of flows in the context of this chapter is that while Castells sees news media as playing an important role in all social action, he does not consider this to be one of power. Rather, he considers the media to be a door through which the contestants for power pass en route to battle (Couldry and Curran, 2003). Additionally, Massey (1994) articulates the "power geometry" (pp. 149–150) of time-space compression – referenced in our introduction – which refers to how social groups and individuals are placed in distinct ways in relation to flows and interconnections.

Massey argues that those of the news media are among those who hold influential positions in social flows and movement and can use time-space compression to their advantage. To be a news "node" in which information relevant to a particular social context is expected to pass represents a type of power worth protecting. But this form of power can only ever truly be effective if there is meaning ascribed to the space by individuals in the first instance.

Place and "sense of place"

Talk of space and flows almost inevitably leads to discussion about place, where social meaning is ascribed to "space". The more the world shrinks,

The trichotomy in digital journalism studies 25

after all, the more the idea of place takes center stage, for "without physical barriers to interaction what matters more is access to the right places with the right people" (Schragger, 2016, p. 25).

Castells makes the point that the "space of flows" does not permeate down through the whole realm of human experience in the network society, as the overwhelming majority of people live in places and so perceive their space as "place-based" (Castells, 2010, p. 453). Certainly, places can be physical or virtual (Lemos, 2010), but are ultimately determined where a person or a group projects their values (Duarte, 2017). The size, scale, and materiality of "place," therefore, can vary from a comfortable armchair, to a mountain view, entire city, or website. Each of them is considered a perspective of "place," but the degree of significance of each element to one's daily life may differ.

Our "sense of place," meanwhile, emerges when we feel an attachment to or develop a series of behaviors and practices (some embodied) that makes us feel like a "fish in water" rather than a "fish out of water." Bourdieu (1984) conceptualized this process as the "habitus" within a given social space that often manifests within physical (or digital) places of cultural meaning.

Our sense of place is often strongly associated with and linked to physical surroundings, to people, even objects, artifacts, and digital sites; "place" is a deep feeling of comfort, ease, and familiarity or a connection we can't always explain. When such feelings and actions become deeply internalized, there is significant advantage to those whom are considered custodians of or holding influence over such places. In fact, certain individuals and institutions, including news media, are expected to perform this role (Bourdieu, 1984; Hess, 2017a). For example, reporters within the journalistic field develop a range of practices or build a feel for the game within newsrooms, even embodied cultural knowledge about the geographic areas that become their "patch" for reporting, and they gain credibility and legitimacy among audiences for this type of knowledge (Hess and Waller, 2017).

Mobility is important here because in a transient world we may develop multiple senses of place, regardless of our location at any given moment. While digital media may create a tangible disconnect between physical space and social space, this does not mean we possess no "sense of place" at all (Meyrowitz, 1985), particularly in virtual spaces or in our imaginations of what some places and spaces might be.

Media coverage, and the news media's perceived connection to serving spaces, "massively multiplies the interconnections between places, rather than weakening our sense of place" (Couldry, 2000, p. 30). But a sense of place may take time to develop in any geographic environment. Tuan (1977) contends embodied knowledge and practices that shape and are shaped by

26 *The trichotomy in digital journalism studies*

our sense of place take time to develop and can be expressed physically as well as psychologically.

Mediated sense of place and news media as a "place"

Increasingly, journalism scholars are studying the ways news media help to facilitate or serve as symbolic totems to "places" – especially geographic territory such as small towns and cities (Gutsche, 2014a; 2017; Hess and Waller, 2017). The term "mediated sense of place," meanwhile, has also been applied in broader media and communications scholarship to explore the effects our digital media experiences have on shaping our "sense of place," especially when it comes to understanding physical locales and geographic terrain.

Bork-Huffer (2017), for example, found that in order to gain an understanding of places with which people are not familiar, they use digital technologies such as Facebook and Google Maps to get a "feel for a place" while news media are adopted as a source for place attachment and "to get involved" in a specific geography (p. 2163). Others have also highlighted the importance of the material turn when it comes to understanding news in the digital age, such as newsroom editorial office buildings and printed newspapers, as sites where people develop a strong sense of attachment or place.

Usher (2018a) argues that news buildings (think *The Wall Street Journal, The New York Times,* or the fictional *Daily Planet*) have come to represent "places" of authoritative and legitimate news production and are imbued with the values associated with the journalistic field. Usher contends that journalists have associated a decline in the size and scope of newsrooms and news buildings in the digital age as a sign of the delegitimization of the profession across wider social space.

Moores (2012), meanwhile, suggests there has been a strong association between newspaper reading and the idea of "place," because the very practice of reading a newspaper – folding it on the subway, wiping ink from fingertips – becomes so familiar.

Moores make the important point that people require considerable repetition in their media and news interactions and return to media artifacts in order to form lasting attachments to places. In other words, news users take their time with this form of media. Yet, there is an increasing failure within journalism studies to slow the tempo in discussions about news production in the digital age.

In capitalist societies, where a neo-liberal doxa (see next chapter) is reinforced, time is money, and so when it comes to the news media, "fast time" is seen as productive time: think 24-hour news cycles, by-the-minute social

The trichotomy in digital journalism studies 27

media tweets for breaking news, or "news now" models imposed by major media conglomerates.

The idea of allowing news habits to evolve among audiences, to appreciate the context in which they develop and foster familiarity and new ritualistic behavior within new spaces and "places" of news is not widely considered in a period of digital disruption. Our own research demonstrates the importance of generating and appreciating familiar environments for news users in both print and digital spaces, at a time when about the only thing consistent in online news spaces is the brand or masthead.

Consider this comment from a local news editor of a small Australian newspaper about making the shift from print to online spaces who spoke in a 2016 interview about the potential of local newspapers to shape daily life.

> We actually deliberately decided to put up PDF copies of the printed paper online, especially for things like births, deaths, and marriage notices rather than put them into a new looking digital format. People were familiar with this and it's too much for them to be expected to make the entire shift to digital where everything looks different. Lots of other city journalists would think we were a bit backward doing that rather than keeping up with the times, but we knew it's what our readers wanted.

This insight from the local level gives us a nuanced understanding of people's connection to the news "in place," particularly when the local news pages, or entire papers, focus on meanings of our lives – and deaths.

Morley (2000) highlights, for example, our "sense of place" is evident in both life and death, with many bodies returned to places of significance for burial or the scattering of ashes (p. 32). The practice of putting a death notice in a local paper, for example, continues to be an unspoken rule of engagement for many in both Eastern and Western cultures and highlights news media's connection to people's sense of place (Hess, 2015).

Daily – and non-daily – news users have highlighted they will pay to publish death notices in newspapers that serve as an intermediary to places of significance where they live, work, or have developed social connections. Interviews with funeral parlors in local communities in Australia, for instance, highlight that idea. Said one parlor operator:

> The first thing we actually do is ask them (grieving relatives or friends) about newspaper advertisements. So we offer the local paper and the out-of-town papers as well, but the local paper is always first. Ninety-five percent of people put a notice in and it doesn't matter about age or class.
>
> (Hess, 2017b, p. 18)

28 *The trichotomy in digital journalism studies*

Intersections of media power, sense of place, and as we shall soon discuss, territory, are evident in such sections of the newspaper that announce both births and deaths, yet such dimensions of the news are given short shrift in journalism studies, generally. Nevertheless, it is through such powerful rituals that we can also begin to appreciate the very "sense of place" that is established through engagement with news objects – such as newspapers and their designated sections and how these elements are integrated into non-news practices, such as in a funeral parlor.

Indeed, interviews with editors and everyday audiences highlight that when funeral notices cannot be found to be "in their usual place" such as in digital spaces, audiences can become agitated and the magical power that has them unquestionably engage in such practices of viewing such aspects of the everyday is lifted (Hess, 2015).

Such a sense of place created in the news can generate significant advantage for certain news providers over others. The ability to transform digital spaces into "places" of meaning for audiences, or to serve as an intermediator to the places that matter to people most, is a useful thought for news media players looking to remain sustainable and viable in the digital era that continues to complement, challenge, or replace print.

For notions of geographic territory to evolve in cultural interpretations of space and place, then, there must be a set of distinct rules, routines, and patterns imposed by the powerful to which users adapt in ways that make their territory "theirs" (Duarte, 2017). An appreciation of the trichotomy of "space," "place," and "territory" provides much greater scope to engage with the development of meaning, practices, and time around sites of news competition. And it is within notions of the territory where issues of control, power, surveillance, rituals, cultural values, and capital appear.

Unpacking media territory

Morley (2000; 2006) argues that the instinct to preserve an identity of territory and to defend it is one of the deepest and strongest implanted in mankind. Territory has traditionally been linked to political demarcation of a geography and has wrongly been considered to be simply synonymous with the mapping of geography (Deleuze and Guattari, 1988; Massey, 1994).

Of course, assemblage theory is not our preferred mode of inquiry here. In digital spaces, a very primitive view of new media territory might evolve with the click of a computer mouse via the purchase of a "domain name" and URL address.

While digital space, then, is an abundance of unchartered territory, it is important to highlight that territorial practices only gain power when we ascribe meaning to places that others lay claim to. Territory depends on the

The trichotomy in digital journalism studies 29

ability of the powerful to enact common practices, values, rituals, morals, and rules that overlay a space or place. Boundary maintenance, then, may be key to establishing different degrees of access to people, things, and relationships, yet boundaries alone do not fully determine the success of territorial practices around places.

Those who move into a territory temporarily find that they, too, must submit to certain rules and practices, all of which determine appropriate behavior expected of members (Duarte, 2017). This social behavior, in a cycle of maintenance by institutional forces, including discourse perpetuated by news media, reinforces people's behavior, reinstating the territory as the rightful way of appropriating that portion of space.

News media, we suggest, have been more focused on erecting paywalls and generating binaries between audiences in terms of access to economic capital and internet resources rather than fostering new cultural rites of passage and a sense of inclusion for audiences. It is our contention, therefore, that the formation of news media territory is multi-layered and features three interconnecting dimensions: (1) at the meta-level, the perceived custodianship of place (currently understood as journalist as agent of public sphere[s]), (2) a dependence on other institutions of power such as the state and judiciary to reinforce news territory, and (3) the ability to mediate our connection to and shape values, rules, and ritualistic practices.

In the sections that follow, we draw much more closely on the relationship between news media and Facebook – its behemoth and controversial status today making it a centerpiece for critiquing interactions between users, news, sociability, and policies – to consider these interconnecting dimensions of territory in media spaces.

Zuckerberg's Facebook creation, with its slogan "connects you with the people around you," has become a billion-dollar empire with more than one billion active users worldwide at a time when the traditional business model sustaining news has crumbled. The trichotomy of place, space, and territory is a necessary one as the battle lines are drawn among those jostling to position themselves as central to our social worlds.

Digital public sphere as territory?

At a meta-level, journalists in Western democracies increasingly and insistently reinforce their custodianship of the public sphere in digital spaces. At first glance, positioning the public sphere as "territory" might appear to be an oxymoron, especially given that the public sphere is celebrated as a space in which people "come together" freely to debate politics for the benefit of a collective, while the emphasis of territory is on power and control, in- and out-groups.

30 *The trichotomy in digital journalism studies*

Yet one of the great, often continued fallacies of the 21st Century is the idea that the news media, and the internet itself, offer a free and safe public space for all, a space for participation and conversation independent of power relations and territorial practices. Terms and concepts familiar to journalism studies scholars, like "public sphere" or "network society," initially sound like they are closely attuned to such complexities of space, but often journalism scholarship that relies on such notions de-emphasizes these aspects for other considerations (Peters, 2015).

How the doxic idea of the professional journalist (see Chapter 3) is reinforced at a time when everyone and anyone can lay claim to new digital territory warrants attention here. It is within this context, for example, that the wheels of boundary work have been furiously turning as scholars focus on the way journalists enact ideals of trust and professionalism and the connection to the public sphere to reassert who and what makes a journalist in the digital age (Carlson and Lewis, 2015).

In carving out digital media territory, Facebook executives have made their intentions clear that they do not wish to position the social media juggernaut as agent of the public sphere. In the debate about fake news and influence upon the 2016 US presidential election, Facebook was clear that it was not a news outlet (Gutsche, 2018).

Facebook's specific responses have been reiterated to Parliamentary inquiries, US Congressional hearings, and to media reports across the globe that it is in the business of connecting people socially, not politically – a point of distinction we shall return to soon. In the United States, for example, the foundations of the Fourth Estate fortified by the First Amendment, rest on the importance of the press as a watchdog, a civic forum, and as an institution of agenda-setting that holds the powerful to account and that is bound by long-standing liability laws (Buni, 2016). By contrast, the foundations of Facebook rest in large part on the provision of the Communications Decency Act's (1996) Section 230(c), or the Good Samaritan Act, which reads: "No provider or user of an interactive computer service shall be treated as the publisher or speaker of any information provided by another information content provider."

Journalists themselves hover between the burden of and the perceived respectability that comes with its commitment to serving the public sphere. On one hand, they claim there is no longer a level economic playing field between themselves and social media, because Facebook is not subjected to the same terms, conditions, and expectations imposed by other institutions of power. In turn, they lobby for Facebook to be subjected to the same rules and regulations that apply in their own media and legal territories guided by defamation laws, copyright, social responsibility, and paradigm maintenance of the journalistic interpretive community.

The trichotomy in digital journalism studies 31

Yet, on the other hand, journalists draw on tried and tested norms and values of trust, truth, and accuracy as a symbolic arsenal (a key feature of territorial practices) to distinguish themselves from other new players in digital spaces that are applied to reinforce their custodianship of the public sphere. This is exemplified, of course, by accusations that Facebook has been complacent in facilitating the rise of fake news (McNair, 2018) and fueled by news of Facebook selling private data for political purposes during the 2018 Cambridge Analytica scandal, in which individuals' private data on Facebook was sold to bolster US President Donald Trump's election campaign (Kleinman, 2018).[2]

Beyond the public sphere: Territorial battles in the social sphere

In order for those in power to claim territory, they must, of course, develop the legitimacy in which to reinforce certain values and ritualistic practices. While the journalistic field is focused on its reputation in patrolling its role in the public sphere, the exponential rise of Facebook highlights to us the rapid accumulation of symbolic and imaginative power that emerges from within the wider social sphere.

We argue elsewhere (Hess and Gutsche, 2018) that there is a need to examine more closely the binary between the public sphere and the idea of the wider social sphere in journalism studies. Whereas the public sphere focuses on politics, public debate, and participation, the social sphere emphasizes collectivity, sociability, connection, issues of morality, and ritual.

Facebook's rising dominance in the social sphere (one that bridges geographies) has highlighted the powerful interplay between social and public worlds and the interdependent relationship between the two. It raises an important question for journalism studies in the digital age: "What if journalism, in its obsession with the public sphere, has been patrolling and preserving too narrow a territory?" As Australian journalist Nick Feik (2017) contends, while Facebook and Google may be responsible for the collapse of the traditional business model of news, "blaming them is like holding a shark responsible for biting" (Feik, 2017). What is the blame to be associated with journalism itself?

Ethological studies tell us that when other animals from the same species enter a particular space they will eventually notice this to be a region claimed by another individual or group (Hall, 1959). Facebook was, however, considered an entirely different species by news media when it first appeared as the new kid on the media block in 2004. The platform was novel to journalists who tolerated and even played and experimented with it. News outlets across the Western world readily adopted the mantra, "Visit

32   *The trichotomy in digital journalism studies*

our Facebook page." In fact, they continue to do so, using it as a space in which to locate and engage with news sources, to develop a more transparent audience base, and to "engage" with users.

What is overlooked in discussions about journalism and social media, particularly related to Facebook and its cousin, Twitter, is the evolution of media symbolic and imaginative power (see next chapter) that these platforms "just are," rather than acknowledging the temporal and historical dimensions of how it came to "be." News media has, for example, established legitimacy in the societies it serves not only from its important role within the public sphere, but its influential role in facilitating social connections within physical places that has been established over time (Hess, 2015).

The ability to connect people to each other and people to place, forming ideas of collective identity and of social order, tend to take a backseat in journalism studies but are integral to the trichotomy of place, space, and territory, and require not to be forgotten. Early newspapers, for example, have perhaps always served as an intermediary to people's sense of place. In colonial Australia and America, for instance, newspapers played a vital role in building a sense of community among new settlers but also kept people connected to their distant homelands by providing news from abroad. Shipping notices, births, deaths, and marriage notices, court appearances, and places for rent dominated the front page of news prior to the 20th Century, long before the rise of the professional journalist.

In the decades that followed, radio and television was celebrated, too, not just for the new ability to bridge space and time in the reporting of matters of public interest, but for the newfound ability to enact family rituals within the home and build an imagined sense of national cohesion (Anderson, 1983). The point we make here is that despite being perceived as two different species, both Facebook and news media evolved from what is now the center of highly contested territory in the digital world – the social sphere.

Dependence on other institutions of power to shape territorial boundaries

While news media have been both celebrated and lamented for their adversarial – and at times contentious – relationship with the political field, big news media players have turned to the state to have the territorial lines redrawn in order to curb the rising power of Facebook. As highlighted earlier, it is important to understand that the study of news media territories moves beyond issues of media ownership and government regulation, but this dimension is certainly important, nonetheless, to examining how media territories evolve and are maintained and challenged.

The trichotomy in digital journalism studies   33

While news media outlets often align their circulation or news "territory" to particular geographic areas, the center of these zones often aligns neatly with politically constructed regions such as states, nations, or local government boundaries or boroughs. Australia's news media system for example, is mirrored on a three-tiered political structure of national, state, and local. Governments, too, also possess power in many countries to control exactly how much media territory an individual media proprietor can claim as their own, and in communist countries such as Vietnam and China the government may elect to control media territory in its entirety.

The level of political influence, nonetheless, in the shaping of territory and in reinforcing the legitimacy of certain news media providers over others, can be both subtle and overt and can have powerful implications for journalism practice. Consider the role of the Australian Communications and Media Authority that is entrusted with constructing and defining that country's "local" news zones in which commercial broadcasters serve. Rather than align with municipal boundaries, these zones are shaped at the discretion of the statutory authority and group dozens of small towns and cities separated by vast geographic distance within the same "local area" (see Australian Communications Media Authority).

In countries such as the United States, the United Kingdom, and Australia, there is also dispute over the most legitimate channels in which to direct government advertising spending, which has represented uncontested and substantial revenue for traditional newspapers for centuries (Hess, forthcoming; Weber, 2008). It is now a practice that is being challenged in the digital era.

Such funding, which has long been considered a consistent and dominant form of advertising revenue for mainstream news media (as well as fulfilling a legal obligation of government to share information with the masses), also represents influence that is much more powerful and uneven as municipalities continue to be required under legislation to publish notices in a local newspaper. This is despite the plethora of new information channels potentially available to councils to direct such spending.

An inability to tap into this source, for example, can leave a new hyperlocal start-up venture parched for funding while long-serving local newspapers are guaranteed sustenance. There is growing concern, too, within local government ranks that maintaining the status quo around public notice expenditure may not provide the optimum conditions to enhance local democracy. This dependence upon institutions outside of journalism itself reveals the complexities of how territory is formed, what influences the interests and needs of journalists to shape a sense of a single "community," and how and why journalists cover what they do in ways that they do and where they do.

34 *The trichotomy in digital journalism studies*

The ability to mediate and shape perceptions around places of meaning

News media hold a long-established history and degree of symbolic power that gives them an advantage over media players such as Facebook in territorializing news zones. As we explore throughout this book, the ability of news outlets to reinforce doxic ideas such as "community," for example, within defined geographic areas is well-documented in journalism scholarship – especially when it comes to the role and place of local media (Gutsche, 2012; Hess and Waller, 2014).

We also highlight in our articulations here that for territories to be maintained, there must be a perception that those who are custodians of such places are serving the interests of a collective, reinforcing shared values and practices if it is to succeed (Hess, 2017a). Territory can be weakened, however, when those in power impose values and rules too far removed from individual perceptions of the place.

A small study of local news in Australia, for example, highlights the rising trend of Facebook's local "I love my town" sites that are filling a space where some locals feel traditional news media are failing – especially when it relates to the generation of shared values and a "sense of community." Qualitative interviews with locals in one Australian municipality suggest that the "I love my town" site is rapidly climbing in membership, even though the "town" is also served by a local newspaper and radio station.

For some, the site became users' "go-to source for local news" where users regularly post images of landscape photography, announce and discuss events in the town, feature job opportunities, and send "Thank you" messages to those who show civic virtue and acts of kindness such as moving fallen tree branches that blocked roads and driveways after a storm. As one resident and "I love my town" user said in an interview in October 2016:

> The newspaper doesn't always reflect the way we feel about the town. There's always bad news, when we'd like to see more of the positive stuff that makes us a community.

And from another user around the same time period in 2016: "Putting up a photo of a sunset or a nice picture of the beach. People just like that and they respond to that."

These examples and the "I love my town" site itself go beyond how users turn to social media to create and maintain networks, but together they are a critique upon traditional and legacy (some would say establishment) journalism. Recent years within which journalism has seen its authority and legitimacy dispersed and diluted across a myriad of outlets' print and broadcast platforms, as well as multiple approaches to be "everything to

The trichotomy in digital journalism studies   35

everyone" on TV, the computer, tablets, phones, social media, and even wearable devices have not, however, coincided with a desire of collectives to recognize themselves outside of their own networks.

The power of community: A constant influence

Forming a sense of collectivity, of social cohesion, has been a key journalistic function across societies, although it takes a backseat to notions of being a watchdog and objectivity in the journalistic field. In the digital world, there is perhaps no better exemplar of the fallacy and power of the community – or of notions of a "single" community – than Facebook's deliberate strategy to build territory in digital spaces, using the shareability, prominence, frequency, and authority of spreadable news.

Originally serving a well-defined group of Harvard University students through its early predecessor of Facemash, Facebook was designed to compare the attractiveness of two Harvard students though voting by the click of a mouse. In the process, a key gap within the university's social sphere was identified, according to one American journalist who cites a close friend of Zuckerberg:

> In creating Facebook, then, Zuckerberg had hit on the school's weakness. Harvard does a lot of things. It churns students through lectures and labs. It launches curricular reviews and stem-cell initiatives; it raises money, and buys up property (or at least, it used to). But Harvard could *not* manufacture community. Facebook could.
>
> (Davis O'Brien, 2010)

Duarte (2017) contends social groups can attempt to turn a place into a territory in order to legitimize themselves to other social groups, converting their values into rules and symbols, while on the other hand existing dominant groups try to soften their rules and symbols, converting them into values to display territory as if it were a place.

Consider, at the most rudimentary level, the role of Facebook with its specialized lexicon and unspoken rules around "liking" and "friending" and the use of letters and numbers to symbolize information exchange on local "buy sell swap" pages that are emerging across the globe (i.e., F = first in line to buy the good, N = next in line). When people don't conform to the rules of the space, it can lead to hostility and defensiveness of those complicit to the territory. Take this comment from a user of a local Facebook buy sell swap page in Australia.

> I've noticed lots of underhanded behavior on this site lately. People don't know what they are doing. Sellers are bypassing people who do

36 *The trichotomy in digital journalism studies*

the decent thing and put themselves in line to purchase (F) and then they just go and sell to anyone. You are not being honest. And just being plain rude. This is not a page rule, but we all know how it works. Be a decent seller. It's not hard? Or get out.

(Warrnambool Buy Sell Swap Facebook page, 2018)

When an individual is newly introduced to such spaces, they assume the role of outsider as they attempt to possess the relevant habitus or "sense of place," a difficult challenge in spaces where unspoken "common sense" and taken-for-granted rules apply. Indeed, this type of social interaction related to newness and conformity resonates with scholarship on media and liminality (Couldry, 2003) as the battle for media territory intensifies.

During liminal periods of all kinds, social hierarchies may be reversed or temporarily dissolved, continuity of tradition may become uncertain, new rites of passage emerge, and future outcomes once taken for granted may be thrown into doubt (Turner, 1988). The battle for media legitimacy then, requires a much broader view of how this takes place both within journalism and media and across wider social spaces.

Herwig (2009), for example, unpacks liminality and "communitas" in the context of social media which illustrates the differences between news and social media in the current digital environment. Herwig highlights how sites such as Facebook are rich with social norms and expectations – from the initial membership sign-up to the use of terms such as "friends" and "followers." As Facebook built "community," however, news media revealed its deep connection to capitalism, prompting an open and urgent dialog around people's need to "pay" for news (an anti-thesis to community-building).

What also has not emerged from the debate about the role of Facebook and its role in sharing the "news" is journalism's continual use of social media to brand, sell, promote, and "engage" with audiences. As of this writing, there have been movements by individuals and some collectives to leave Facebook due to the company's inaction – or action – in releasing profile information for nefarious private and political agendas. Yet no journalistic agency or outlet has done the same as a means by which to distance itself from controversy and, in so doing, the commercial marketplace.

Conclusion

We began this chapter by highlighting the incredibly powerful way that technology is shaping our daily lives through social media and the expansion of sociability beyond the "community-building" of legacy journalism and into the collective spirit of online users. Yet, digital technology is just one part of the picture when assessing today's geographies of journalism.

The trichotomy in digital journalism studies   37

When the motor vehicle became essential to our daily lives, it was clear our practices around mobility had changed dramatically: we could travel great distances in a much shorter timeframe, if and when it was convenient or necessary to do so.

What we cannot lose sight of now, as our bodies become digital via wearables and sensors, and our online profiles learn what we like before we do, is that when we turn on our car engines, we are almost always planning on going "somewhere" even though road maps, sat nav devices, and mobile phones can direct us anywhere and everywhere – even to places we hadn't imagined visiting. Our cars are often garaged with us close to "home," and the roads we take often lead us to and from a particular destination – often so repetitive that we drive in autopilot – we just know where to go.

The problem with digital journalism that we wish to address in future chapters and that is built on foundations of space, place, and territory in this chapter is that journalism studies struggles with the slow-pacedness of understanding the complexities of our geographic awareness and awayness. In other words, and as the next chapter examines, the flash and flair of the digital must be disrupted in times of change to become aware (or [re]aware) of the cultural influences and implications of place-making that direct us away from attacking issues of powers within ideological constructions of geography.

Notes

1 It is important to note that news reporting has always been affected by some form of rapid technological change since even before the 19th Century whether it be the rise of the shipment of news from continent to continent or the invention of the telegram, telephone, radio, or television.
2 Of course, both Facebook and other platforms are accused of attempting to draw and exploit on the values that journalism itself represents. In any type of symbolic warfare, there are always dirty tactics which highlight the cultural values of trust, accuracy, and validity assigned to news media in the battle to preserve news territory in the digital age. New domain names that mimic traditional news sites, for example, have been registered in the hope of drawing on media power to gain legitimacy, before deliberately setting out to deceive audiences. Consider the founder of fake news who set up the site DenverGuardian – which aimed to serve as "a site that could've easily been believable and located it up with real local news stories before sneaking in major fake news stories with national appeal." For more, see https://thehustle.co/fake-news-jestin-coler.

3 Symbolic and imaginative power

From doxa to innovation in journalism

In journalism studies, dominant and popular conversations of how geography works are often simplified versions that bifurcate issues of power, agency, language, and discourse about place. In this chapter, we build on the geographies of journalism by unpacking constructs that help to understand the reporter's role as legitimate place-maker in society – especially the concepts of symbolic and imaginative power.

In the introduction we highlighted the importance of the "spatial turn" in exploring the geographies of journalism with concepts of fields, spheres, and networks. We also touched on Bourdieu's theorization of social spaces as fields, which serve as our tool kit of choice here to further discussions about journalism and place-making. In the following section, we extend Bourdieu's (1989; 2001) notion of symbolic power and the acquiescence to symbolic violence through geographic interpretation. By symbolic power, we mean the often-unquestioned ability of certain legitimate agents in society to construct reality about places that either matter to us or which we only come to understand through mediated representations.

We highlight the importance of "news myth" (Gutsche, 2012; Lule, 2001) alongside the Bourdieusian notion of "doxa" to consider the ideological processes that shape the geographies of journalism and the value of rituals and boundary work in place-making processes. The "imaginative" notion of place, meanwhile, comes into play when we develop an idea in our minds about spaces, places, and people we have never encountered or experienced, and therefore we "imagine" a place to be.

Imaginative power (Ettema, 2005) is important here for understanding the challenge of arguing against traditional, dominant notions of what a place is or might be. The power elements of this ideological work of what and how is imagined is linked in large part to the power of ideologies, structures, and the maintenance and strength of legitimate place-makers (and institutions) that at times resist testing new, innovative ways of seeing the world.

Symbolic power, doxa, and myth

As we have established in Chapter 1, the meaning-making function of journalism is inherent in cultural geography both through representations of reality and the ways that people use media to reinforce their understandings of and connection to places. Bourdieu was not a geographer, but he was interested in how the social world shapes physical spaces. We, among others, argue that an inability to give credence to the non-human dimensions of geography (such as the natural landscape) is a limitation of Bourdieu's conceptual approach (i.e., Hess and Waller, 2014). His theory of symbolic power, nonetheless, is useful because it explores the inherent ways in which the wider field of power (politics) shapes reality or frames the way we see and view places.

To be clear, Bourdieu and Thompson (1991) contend that symbolic power is the:

> power of constituting the given through utterances, of making people see and believe, of confirming and transforming the vision of the world and thus the world itself, an almost magical power which enables one to obtain equivalent of what it obtained through force.
>
> (p. 170)

News media, like the political field, are seen to wield considerable symbolic power – what Couldry (2000) refers to as media power – which can both consciously and unconsciously reinforce dominant attitudes or "doxa" and shape our social practices in a given context. By doxa, we mean the "ordinary acceptance of the usual order which goes without saying and therefore usually goes unsaid" (Bourdieu, 1984, p. 424).

Doxa is important to the geographies of journalism, because such dominant ideas about people and places are often inextricably linked to physical sites of significance – geopolitical divides such as the very acceptance of the need to create borders between countries to the way we often view the notion of "community" to be something tangible and considered synonymous with small towns and cities. Let us first discuss the latter.

Bourdieu (1999) contends socially distanced people find nothing "more intolerable" than physical proximity (p. 128), highlighting how problematic equating "community" with geographic territory can be (see also discussion in Gutsche and Salkin, 2013; Hess and Waller, 2014). It is a fallacy to suggest that everyone within a given geographic space considers themselves as equal or sharing the same social values.

In 2017, the *South China Morning Post*, for example, reported on the rising angst among affluent homeowners in Beijing who were being forced

40 *Symbolic and imaginative power*

to share public facilities with the less wealthy living on their street (Yangpen, 2017). Those in the upper classes had erected physical barriers such as fences and gates around outdoor public spaces and shared facilities to avoid "mingled living." A social housing policy now bans developers from building walls in the interests of promoting a sense of "community," which is an idea encouraged by the politically powerful.

In the introduction, we also highlighted the case of a series of bushfires that ravaged parts of Australia in early 2018. There, the Prime Minister, Malcolm Turnbull, toured the sites of devastation and declared at a press conference:

> When mother nature throws her worst at us time and time again, it brings out the solidarity, the love, the community spirit and the resilience of Australians again and again.
>
> (Houlihan, 2018)

Here we see evidence of the figurehead of Australian politics reinforcing the powerful doxic idea of "community" that he associates not just with a particular town but which is extended to an entire country and perpetuated via media coverage.

We should be clear here that in journalism studies, the discourse that is examined comes from both journalists and those they quote or from whom they are supplied with information, or evidence. However, our contention is the degree to which journalists rely on these comments from officials and sources and the ways in which these comments do not operate significantly differently from the narratives that journalists themselves present in overarching explanations of the world.

Yet, the question for us becomes the degree to which journalists are responsible both for the comments that they select to be included in news texts as well as the explanations that journalists construct from the information provided. In other words, whose text is the news article in which an official source claims a place or a people to be a single "community?" In our view, the text becomes a shared text, one in which the journalist, however, is positioned to make selections and interpretations based on the multiple perspectives and forms of information.

These forms of expression and explanation in journalism extend beyond a single news text into narratives of explanation, overarching positions of "community," definitions of borders and boundaries, and explanations of power relations and social conditions inside and outside of those spaces and places. Such a process is rooted within narrative explanation of societal institutions, of which journalism is one, to provide to people fair representation and governance.

In this system (which is represented in and beyond Western society) certain elite individuals and groups, especially in politics and news media, are

Symbolic and imaginative power 41

considered custodians of civic virtue expected to reinforce such ideals for the purposes of their own legitimacy (Bourdieu, 1984; Hess, 2016).

Hess (2017a), for instance, draws on Bourdieu to argue that a key to understanding journalistic legitimacy in the digital age is the news media's relationship to upholding or being perceived as a custodian of the universal doxic idea of a common good and negotiating its meaning in certain places and contexts. Being perceived as a negotiator and reinforcer of such values is not necessarily an immediate source of destructive force, though these individuals and relationships, as well as the social (laws) and cultural (education) standards upon which a society is built maintains environments within which power is at play. Hess contends:

> There are always those elites in society who reinforce or are seen to stand in for and negotiate these values in a given context which speaks to their very legitimacy in the digital age. Journalism, like the state, wield this power.
>
> (p. 801)

Still, it is the professional or institutional level at which journalists are trained to conform to these power systems – and are taught how to perform within them through use of language and narration, identification and explication of conflict, and basic knowledge of who to go to for information and how to distribute it. Through this training, somehow, the journalist is taught that she is the expert on an issue – or a geography in which an issue is highlighted – if she "goes to" the "right expert," even if she is truly not familiar with the many spheres of possible interpretation in a geographic space where she has never been.

Professional journalism as doxa: The case of the city/country divide

The very belief that journalists are *the authorities* for information-gathering and storytelling in the digital age is itself a powerful "doxic" attitude that has evolved over time. This is being both challenged and reinforced in the digital age, especially in disputes over media territory, which we outlined in the previous chapter. There, too, are cultural binaries interlocked with physical geography that determine the degrees of legitimacy among journalists themselves. That is, a journalist's level of prestige and/or credibility can ultimately depend on where they are located in physical space, such as those who gain a designated seat and the privilege of "witnessing" governmental debates in Washington, London, or Toronto, to the particularly powerful doxic binary between metropolitan and rural journalism practices.

42 *Symbolic and imaginative power*

The city/country divide was one identified quite well by Raymond Williams (1976) and Hebert Gans (2004) and presented elsewhere (Fry, 2003), but until recently has been largely assumed, implied but often left unsaid in journalism scholarship. Nielsen (2015) has contended that local journalism has not been "sexy" while Hess and Waller (2017) suggest it has been given short shrift in journalism studies in favor of examining big media. Consider comments from several local reporters in the United Kingdom and Australia that appeared in media coverage from our home nations or from interviews we have conducted that reinforce this doxic attitude.

British journalist Grace Newton (2013) shared this experience about her work as a small-town reporter on the national media platform *The Guardian* this way: It's perhaps not the setting that many ambitious media students dream of for their job," she said, with part of the problem being "the tendency of journalism courses to steer students towards London and the nationals, the 'glamour' option of the industry." She added, "Following the local path has been the best decision I ever made, and I'd urge any aspiring reporter to seriously consider weekly papers as much more than just a step on the ladder.

An Australian local reporter, meanwhile, offered his views of working in the local news environment in rural Australia as part of a study on the value of local news. His comments highlight the sociability of the local news (Hess and Gutsche, 2018) in ways that advance our argument about divides between "the city and the country." As he said in an interview in September 2016: "I know I'm just a local reporter not some big [city] journo, but I really like what I do and the people you meet."

In both instances and from different corners of the globe, these journalists appear almost apologetic for working in the local media sector and accept themselves as inferior to metropolitan journalists, reinforcing the idea of what we might term as "metropolitan domination" within the journalistic field.[1]

Symbolic violence in mediated "places"

Those positioned as lesser or inferior through the perpetuation of "doxic" attitudes are subjected to what Bourdieu (2001) refers to as symbolic violence – the "invisibilization" of certain individuals or groups which comes through a refusal of legitimate, public existence (p. 119). Meanings imposed by symbolic violence are legitimized by "concealing the power relations which are the basis of its force" (Bourdieu and Passeron, 2000, p. 4). Just as the local journalists above appear through discourse to submit to the very idea that they are not of the same professional standing as big-city

Symbolic and imaginative power   43

journalists, forms of symbolic violence perpetuate through wider social spaces and are often played out in geographic contexts.

Consider these comments from a guest columnist in the *Cedar Rapids Gazette* in Cedar Rapids, Iowa, in response to a black resident who was racially profiled there by employees at a clothing store. Within the op-ed (McCoy-McDeid, 2018), evidence of doxic attitudes prevail:

> I'm a broke single mum who lives on the wrong side of town, but yes, I condemn the horrifying incident with the very breath of my being. . . . Dear Black People in Iowa, leaders or otherwise: I see you. Whether you feel you are in a position to vocalize your frustration at yet the latest transgression against our community, know that your feelings are valid. You matter. And, we belong here.

Here, the woman highlights – in two main ways – dominant attitudes perpetuated within the geographic boundaries of Iowa, a place where journalists have turned to such columnists in recent years to address issues of institutionalized racism (Gutsche, 2014a) and that has struggled as a majority white state with the issues of integrating blacks into daily life (for more, see DeLoach, 2018).

Firstly, the woman succumbs to the very doxic belief that there is a "right" and "wrong" side of town, yet she does not challenge this and unintentionally reinforces this engrained view even as she seems to critique it.[2] Secondly, the author suggests that racial discrimination in terms of geographic delineation is a "transgression against the community" – as if the "community" as a single entity is in fact a tangible reality or would even be inclusive and beneficial for all.[3]

Nonetheless, the use of the comment "community" is interesting here in the possibilities of the interpretation by the author and the meaning of the term, though despite this there is no doubt of the author's intent to use the "journalistic place" as a legitimate and authoritative location to express and demand change.

And even though the author is challenging the doxa of white privilege – "Dear Black people of Iowa . . . I see you" – in this instance, she still complies with, rather than resists, other dominant attitudes connected to the geographic region where she lives and works: That is the power of symbolism in the term and expectation of "community," and in the imagination of utopianism that aligns itself with the "common sense" of racial clarity, egalitarianism, and liberalism.[4]

This suggests that notions of objectivity and trust that have aligned with the doxa of the journalistic field should now make way for place-making,

44   *Symbolic and imaginative power*

myth, and morality in the digital age as points of distinction and critical tools to explore the role of the "professional" journalist. To more fully appreciate this power, we highlight the interrelationship between doxa and myth within the geographies of journalism.

News myth as power tool for place-making

While doxa represents knowledge that is beyond question and which agents tacitly accord, myth (Barthes, 1972) emphasizes the value of the sacred story or type of speech that reaffirms and reproduces ideology in relation to people, material objects, and places. In journalism, news stories are considered the siren song of myths (Lule, 2001) by which journalists perform a powerful meaning-making function to reinforce a collective's values, beliefs, and behaviors. In doing so, cultural myths normalize the ideologies of the ruling or socially privileged.

Gutsche and Salkin (2013; 2016; 2017) have presented several instances of mythical application in local news, especially when they present the complexities and consistencies of using myth to demarcate social and geographic positions of power. The two build largely upon work by Jack Lule (2001) that positions within journalism studies the role of overarching and cross-continental mythical explanations of and for natural disaster, extreme public personalities, and moments of crisis and fear. In their work, they reveal the processes of how mythical archetypes – the creation and implementation of characters with traits of humanity, success, failure, danger, and safety – are used in journalism to embed into news texts social and cultural meaning.

These archetypes, traits, and experiences function to tell story within and among landscapes of environments. A "small-town" where sexual violence occurs represents a threat to the traditions and a sense of "community" that could rarely be foreseen to occur outside the actions of a few "bad apples" and intervention from outside the collective (Gutsche and Salkin, 2016). The deaths of young men in a small city on the banks of the Mississippi River in the US, often at night, reveal the character of a "community" to overcome tragedy and a moment to position the men as either pillars or plagues of a community (Gutsche and Salkin, 2013).

In yet another example (Gutsche and Salkin, 2017) the rural space of Amish country in the US is the scene of religious traditionalism where the murder of Amish youth, breaking the silence and pastoralism of the region, positioned for journalists at three levels of distance to the news event an opportunity to measure and present notions of evil as consistent across expectations of audiences and geographies – in large part of who the victims were (children) and where the crime occurred (quiet countryside). In each

Symbolic and imaginative power 45

of these instances, myth served to align (or realign) dominant explanations and expectations of journalists and audiences to interpret influences of events, issues, and spaces in which "community" may exist.

As Nossek and Berkowitz (2007) highlight, when it comes to producing everyday news journalists work according to core values and pressures from within the field, but when core values in society are threatened – such as by terrorism – journalists switch to a cultural narrative that "moves public mind back towards the dominant cultural order" (p. 691). Myth and doxa, then, point to an ongoing activity of persuasion through which people's practices augment as certain attitudes and perceptions are reinforced by those in positions of power.

Boundary work and ritual in place-making

Whereas doxic attitudes shape perceptions about reality and our everyday lives and myth helps to reinforce the imaginary – good versus evil binaries, heroes, villains, and places within which we play out our realities and dreams of which we cannot actually "see," together, doxa and myth underpin the significance of ritual and boundary work which are also important components of journalism's relationship to place-making in the digital age.

Journalistic boundary work and ritual (Carlson and Lewis, 2015; Morley, 2000) help to explore the role of journalism in shaping center and periphery relations, the patrolling and maintenance of socially constructed boundaries, and the cultural meanings attached to geographic borders and territories amongst everyday people (Gutsche, 2014a). Too often, however, as we highlighted in the introduction, boundary work offers an inward-looking approach around the norms and conventions shaping the journalistic profession rather than its interaction with the physical and social spaces journalism serves.

For example, boundary work is often used to explore how journalists cement their professional standing from others who "claim" to be journalists, such as the distinction between "real" or "fake" news (Gutsche, 2018), rather than examine journalism's interaction and demarcation of geographic places and their boundaries (both physical and digital). As media scholar David Morley (2000) contests:

> There is a long history from the Greeks and Romans in the generation of imagined geographies, in which the members of a society locate themselves at the center of the universe where at the spatial periphery in which they picture threatening monsters and grotesques. The further one goes from the center the more threatening the creatures one encounters.
>
> (p. 141)

46 *Symbolic and imaginative power*

While we do not discount the importance of cosmopolitanism – the orientation of openness and care towards distant others in journalism, it is the relationship between news media and the creation and casting of those on the "periphery" (both spatially and socially) that is a key focus of how we interpret geographies of journalism.

Analyzing media ritual in times of celebration representing shared beliefs enables us to tease out ways in which journalism serves as the legitimate center of our social lives in a period of apparent digital disruption. Carey (1977), arguably America's founder of critical cultural studies, positions the ritual view of communication as:

> not directed toward the extension of messages in space but the maintenance of society in time; not the act of imparting information or influence but the creation, representation, and celebration of shared beliefs.
>
> (p. 419)

Carey's approach to ritual communication and community can also be accused of functionalism, rather than fully embracing the dimensions of power at play in social spheres (Couldry, 2003). Non-functionalist accounts of media rituals have developed that are particularly relevant here, which put media power front and center (Cottle, 2006; Couldry, 2000) and provide scope to explore the role of news media to connect, unite, divide, and affirm notions of both collective identity and social differences.

For this project, we prefer Couldry's (2003) interpretation that:

> Media rituals operate to naturalize the notion of a "mediated social order" within which all specific ideologies must compete, as well as legitimizing the particular representational privilege of the media (as a centralized system for producing and distributing images, information, and opinions).
>
> (p. 46, parentheses in original)

The need to get emotional about journalism

Where myth and ritual meet – via verisimilitude – is what Durkheim refers to as a "primordial activity," which holds society together, maintains social systems, and reinforces norms and virtues, especially in times of trauma and crisis. Emotive (or affective) responses by audiences to moments of crisis or celebration also evolve through exposure to journalism and its ritual function. News coverage following the 9/11 terrorist attacks to capture a sense of US patriotism, for instance, focused not only on the grief of three

Symbolic and imaginative power 47

locations, but enhanced a sense of collective "being" of those who were not there.

Emotion has not been traditionally seen as key to good citizenship within public sphere explanations, but scholars have advocated for its attention (Pantii, 2010; Wahl-Jorgensen, 2013). Rather than reinforce moral universalism, Facebook, for example, has turned to the power of emotion to generate its own boundaries within its constructed "community" of users at a time when there is public concern about data protection, fake news, and surveillance of users. In asserting its rising legitimacy in the social sphere (and to keep state regulators at bay), for instance, Facebook banned alt-right group Britain First from accessing the site after its leaders were jailed for anti-Muslim hate crimes in the UK (Hern and Rawlinson, 2018).

Here, Facebook draws upon deep-seated emotional tactics in constructing its boundaries around "acceptable" and "non-acceptable" practices and ideas, focusing on the cultural construct of "hate." A spokesperson for Facebook said it did not remove pages "just because some people don't like them" and allowed controversial political opinions. "But political views can and should be expressed without hate," a corporate statement added (Hern and Rawlinson, 2018). "There are times though when legitimate political speech crosses the line and becomes hate speech designed to stir up hatred against groups in our society," Facebook representatives noted.

The role of emotion in the social sphere and its connection to collective identity and virtue should not be overlooked in discussions of place-making either, such as "real" emotion and "expected" emotion in given contexts. From feelings of personal pride, embarrassment, and grief to shared emotions around sense of belonging, journalism's ritualistic function – and the emotional connection this generates – guides approved behaviors, language, explanations, and relationships that inform public, social life.

The imaginative power of place in journalism studies

Peters and Broersma (2017) argue that in the changing media environment, we need to study new everyday news habits, along with "de-ritualizations and re-ritualizations" (p. 13) if we want to understand what journalism is, or more to the point what it might be, in the changing media environment. For this, we turn to the imaginative power of place that occurs within journalism. For media to wield imaginative power, it must already possess a degree of symbolic power. Imaginative power differs in that it serves as the power to imagine what we cannot see, to create ideas and perceptions that are entirely unreal, and to imagine the authority assigned to meanings of dominant ideologies.

48 *Symbolic and imaginative power*

It is not our intention to wade into the very construct and depths of the imaginary and the imagination that has been debated across the health sciences and philosophy traditions for centuries. Plato, for example, argued works of imagination were non-didactic, and in early Greek thought the imagination was dismissed as unproductive, because it contributed nothing practical to the realm of the polis and was too far removed from reason (Kearney, 2003).

In more contemporary thought, Lacan's notion of the symbolic, the real, and the imaginary and its psycho-analytical significance has been argued to be not too far removed from Bourdieu's theories of social life (Steinmetz, 2006). It is Benedict Anderson's (1983) notion of "imaginative communities," however, that is most cited in journalism studies, as he drew on the creative imaginary to argue that all communities are "imagined" and wield political importance, especially in constructing ideas of nationalism, shared social values, and as media as functioning within a "public sphere."

It is necessary to make clear here that while we acknowledge the cultural and socio-political significance of the imaginary, its role within the geographies of journalism extends beyond a celebration of the discursive forms through which nations and communities imagine themselves into being. Our grounding of imaginative power, rather, sits with scholars such as Ricoeur (1992) and Ritivoi (2006) who align the imaginary with doxa and myth.

On the one hand, imaginative power can be celebrated as something new and innovative, a creative idea we have not considered before. Yet on the other – and increasingly in digital space – we "imagine" ideas about people and places of which we have no concrete sensory experiences (such as Morley's monsters and grotesques who live on the periphery of our social worlds).

As Habermas (1984) rightfully highlights, for example, mythical and ritualistic reinforcement by social elites can impede innovative and critical thought, and so a more critical lens is necessary in understanding journalism and imaginative power in the digital age. Doss (2002), for example, highlights that for the news media, stories of the Oklahoma City bombings and Columbine High School killings in the US became public expressions of grief rather than discussions about the social causes (such as school bullying) or public policies (such as gun control) (Li, 2017). This shrinking of geographies to a single state – and a single state of mind – represents the imaginative power of the press to alter notions of space, place, location, and territory when doing so benefits the dominant audience and power system.

Appadurai (2001) suggests that it is through the imagination that "modern citizens are disciplined and controlled – by states, markets, and their powerful interests" (p. 6). The more symbolic power those who imagine something to be, the more likely they will be to succeed in challenging

Symbolic and imaginative power 49

existing, dominant doxic attitudes over time. On the reverse, those who conform to the dominant interpretation maintain the power of those ideas and the violence of the symbolic battle over meaning.

Consider the rise of the #MeToo movement in 2017 and 2018 which challenges sexual assault and harassment in the workplace. Here, we see the often unspoken doxa of masculine domination (Bourdieu, 2001) labeled and brought into the public arena, largely via mainstream entertainment media. The campaign began 10 years earlier in 2007 (Johnson and Hawbaker, 2018) but wasn't popularized until late 2017 when *The New York Times* engaged in investigative journalism to reveal that dozens of female actresses were accusing Hollywood heavyweight Harvey Weinstein of sexual abuse over decades (Peiser, 2018).

The subsequent journalistic exclusives with high-profile sources, largely spread over social media, generated an accumulation of immense capital within two geographical cities of New York and Hollywood – which themselves represent sites of global symbolic power. The undoing of Weinstein, meanwhile as he turned himself into police in New York in 2018, required a new storytelling approach and a shift in mythical archetypes.

Here, the fusion from social geography to cultural geography is clear. Journalists moved from narratives of cosmopolitan kings and princesses to an evil villain, portraying the Weinstein affair as "The making of a monster" (Johnson and Galloway, 2018) and "Bringing down a monster in Hollywood" (Dowd, 2017). In the process, journalists established themselves as the legitimate authorities by which to judge and establish rule of law, largely ignoring, of course, bigger social and cultural issues of hegemonic masculinity, which are strong within the wider media sphere – including journalism (North, 2009).[5]

Conclusion: Re-imagining the role (and place) for journalism

Appadurai (2001) highlights that while imaginative power is driven by elites, it is also the faculty through which collective patterns of dissent and new designs for collective life emerge. The latter promotes engagement with the sociological imagination (Mills, 2000) in journalism studies, especially in the context of place-making.

The very power of place-making may not be a dominant doxic attitude within the journalistic field itself, but in wider social spaces journalism's influence often goes without saying. This highlights the importance of reflexivity in news practices, which encourages those in the media to interrogate their own social and geographic location and disentangle how this may have shaped their interpretation of a place.

50 *Symbolic and imaginative power*

Indeed, the frequent lack of such reflexivity and the inward-looking observations in journalism studies scholarship that seeks social justice and change through increased citizen participation and public involvement in communication hinders the ability of scholarship to hold open court for creating a just society (Hess and Gutsche, 2018).

Imaginative power also helps us to position – to imagine – what journalism might be as a practice for analyzing and producing innovation and the imagining of places rather than merely consolidating existing beliefs and reinforcing accepted positions within places (Ritivoi, 2006).[6] If Bourdieu helps us to explain why beliefs and practices do not change and how the appearance of change is often the cover for more of the same, concepts such as imaginative power of place may provide a useful counterbalance in rethinking journalism's relationship to societal innovation in the future.

To be clear, much scholarship on innovation as it relates to the journalistic imagination focuses on the way journalists can work with technology to improve co-production of stories or bolster new start-up ventures rather than position innovation as the way in which journalism might understand or help us to re-imagine places for the betterment of society. Existing scholarship does, however, rightfully highlight that innovation in any form can be stifled by long-standing rules and conventions shaping the field, along with a demanding 24-hour news cycle that provides little scope for reflexivity.

Pavlik (2013), meanwhile, argues innovation in the news media should be guided by four principles: intelligence or research, a commitment to freedom of speech, a dedication to the pursuit of truth and accuracy in reporting, and ethics. Our call is for an examination of journalism's innovative role in rethinking "wicked problems" (Lehtola and Ståhle, 2014), especially social justice issues that are not always prominent in the public sphere and by investigating the way people use journalism to connect to others and to place.

We perhaps, then, align our view of innovation with that of Axel Bruns (2014) who contends that media innovation is more than just advancements in media technology as it reflects and promotes desires for societal change. He contends:

> the shift towards a more widespread participation of ordinary users as active content creators and media innovators, make it all the more important to investigate in detail these interlinked, incremental, everyday processes of media and societal change – media innovations are almost always also user innovations.
>
> (p. 13)

In the next chapter, we discuss the processes by which journalists use the imagination of space and place and the justification of their own legitimacy

Symbolic and imaginative power 51

and authority to shape and maintain dominant demarcations of space and interpretations place.

Notes

1 Furthermore, as much scholarship has examined and we have touched upon previously, "the city" has largely been cast as masculine, industrial, and of the "future" in literature and media studies, while "the country" is a place of tradition, substance, and femininity.

2 To be clear, we do not wish to blame the writer for this process of place-making. This divide is her experience and one that has been represented in research about a changing Iowa. But moreover, her experience need not be justified by us. Instead, we are interested in how spatial divides are interpreted and expressed in ways that are normalized and justified or rationalized by experience. In fact, the idea of this divide is acknowledged and provided legitimacy by journalists in the publication of the article itself.

3 We are unsure from the text alone what the author means by "community" and the degree to which her application is to a single population's or demographics' interpretation of a defined "community" or whether she is referring to a geographic space as being representative of a single definition of "community."

4 That journalism functions in a ritualistic manner to create senses of commonality has been well established and continues to plague scholarship on issues of media power and control by downplaying influences that create hegemonic discourse and news coverage, including in the strive for journalistic authority in the digital age.

5 We acknowledge some other movements such as the "Shitty Media Men List" in the US and a series of articles by a former high-profile mainstream (now freelance) journalist exposing alleged sexual harassment in the media and entertainment industry in Australia in 2017 and 2018. Each has gained traction through mainstream media – the latter for example was the product of long-running investigative journalism in conjunction with other traditional providers, rather than the force of social media.

6 To demonstrate a connection between doxa and imagination, Ritivoi (2006) defines imagination "as a volitional act (rather than as a faculty) with social consequences" (p. 52). According to Ritivoi, imagination not only examines and critiques existing doxa, but helps to create and reinforce new doxa. "Imagination, then," Ritivoi writes, "can be seen as an intentional act of consciousness" (p. 56). She continues: "Imagination explores the way in which rhetorical agents can challenge and change the assumptions of their communities in order to allow new arguments and ideas to be heard" (p. 51).

4 Demarcating news space(s) in digital news

Urban sprawl is reshaping many cities across the Western world as new residential subdivisions and cul-de-sacs continue to emerge in response to population growth, rising housing prices around city centers, and the racialized fear of city cores. This movement has created a challenge for city and local governments in building (or fabricating) a sense of social cohesion and collective identity for new residents who call these suburbs home.

For example, in 2018, Bloomington, Minnesota city officials called on residents to help draw and name new neighborhood boundaries in the interests of civic life to better present a notion of a cohesive, but diverse, community (Otarola and Covington, 2018). A completed map was shared with media company Nextdoor, using the online platform as a way to connect people with one another and to reinforce the new zones. As a result, *The Star Tribune* in Minnesota reported that neighbors are now hosting street parties, picking leaders, passing around petitions, and showing up at city hall to speak on issues that may affect them.

The idea of "naming" neighborhoods has been a touchy subject, nonetheless. Several decades earlier, a developer caused a rift between the West and the East sections of the city when he used the phrase "prestigious west Bloomington" to sell houses. Such naming, as in other cities and regions around the world, has been rooted in perceived (and, for some, real) differences and similarities that establish collective identities. Frequently, these collectives exist as much to divide themselves from other spaces and people as they do to create cohesion.

In the simple-most (and possibly naïve) perspective, journalism finds itself at the center of these debates over space, names, territories, and collective identities. Pressured by audiences and advertisers, journalists cover their spaces in ways that are most popular and that result in the least amount of conflict in their assumption of legitimacy and authority to be dominant explainers of everyday life.

Demarcating news space(s) in digital news   53

A more complicated position of journalistic place-making suggests that demarcation and characterization of space and place is a hegemonic act on the part of collaboration between journalists and fellow institutions to maintain power positions over the ways in which the public discusses geography and addresses (perceived) social conditions through public policy, economic decisions, and policing (Gutsche, 2017).

Whichever position one subscribes to, how journalists demarcate spaces – city neighborhoods, regions of countries, political boundaries, and virtual spaces – is a process that is under constant consideration and redefinition. As neighborhoods that were once "bad" become gentrified and "good" – sometimes relying on the notion of badness to earn a hip, quasi-dangerous, or "saved" space (Shumow and Gutsche, 2016) – journalists must alter how they describe events in those spaces and the spaces themselves.

Negotiating new boundaries, such as in the Bloomington case, highlight how elites with symbolic power in society demarcate or reinforce dominant boundaries in the interests of establishing social order or for advantage. Bloomington locals appear not to have questioned the role of City Hall in generating new neighborhoods – nor did they question news media for reinforcing those assumed rights and borders – but officials did bring the authority of a real estate agent into question when he used the label of "prestige" to define space that did not align with public perception or the shared imagination. It is this kind of border-watching that journalists play in physical and digital worlds, of which this chapter is concerned.

Demarcating space: News zones in physical and digital geographies

In the previous chapter, we outlined some of the conceptual tools that help to understand journalism as a legitimate institution of place-making in geographic and digital spaces, notably the ideas of symbolic and imaginative power. Together with doxa, ritual, and myth, they construct or reinforce dominant attitudes or imagine – even re-imagine – places in physical and digital environments.

But more work is needed to understand the way journalists demarcate the physical boundaries in which they generate news in the first instance, before territories evolve and rules and ritualistic practices are cemented. Here, we pay specific attention to news media and the demarcation of space in physical geography, that is – the neighborhoods, suburbs, towns, and cities where we live, work, and play – as a sometimes forgotten or understated starting point in complicating news in digital spheres. We then discuss the

54 *Demarcating news space(s) in digital news*

characterization of these zones in the context of cultural geography and the relationship to the symbolic and imaginary power of place.

Defining news zones

A zone is typically defined in geography studies as an area or stretch of land that has a particular purpose or use, unlike territory which is considered a space under the jurisdiction of a ruler or a perceived authority. Within news zones, therefore, journalists concentrate on sourcing news without being distracted by irrelevant aspects outside the demarcated environment (that is an identified physical or social space).

Often, these demarcated spaces are socio-spatial; most mainstream news outlets tend, for example, to align themselves with specific geographic areas. This doesn't mean news can't be sourced or produced outside the zone, but a zone's journalism must serve the interests of those who share a sense of place or connection within these physical or social spaces, regardless of their degree of mobility and where they may "be" when they access the news (Shoemaker and Reese, 2014).

The boundaries of these zones are not often clearly defined by media operators themselves, which creates issues and news gaps especially at their peripheries. In fact, various media outlets can exist within the same news zones (setting up a battle over territory). The generation of zones is often an initial stage of the journalistic place-making process, and as the zones are almost always socio-spatial, journalists in these zones are dependent on factors such as scale/range, resources, proximity, and distance.

Scale/range, correspondents, and cultural markers

The demarcation of local news media zones begins not with the question "Who is my audience?" but often by assessing issues of scale and reach. Mainstream and hyperlocal news outlets serving suburbs, towns, and cities, for example, often assess what geographic distance they can reasonably cover based on the amount of resources available. Savvy digital media players such as Netflix, have returned to geographic borders to define news territory and control user access. For example, to cut off VPN users from accessing content from its international catalogs, Netflix now prevents users from circumventing "geo-blocks" that enable users to tap into its international library of movies, instead forcing audiences to use locally targeted services available in their geographic region (Rielly, 2016).

While information published via an online platform may now be accessible from "anywhere" and "anytime," most news zones generated by traditional mainstream news providers do tend to overlay or align with political

Demarcating news space(s) in digital news 55

borders (boroughs and municipalities) and with natural ones (rivers and oceans). The exact boundaries are at times unclear, however, and depend on social geography factors such as media ownership, regulation, and resourcing.

In Western and Asian countries such as America, Australia, and Indonesia, commercial broadcasting licenses are issued by governments and are aligned to specific geographic zones.[1] In Australia, for example, news outlets are further required to meet the news needs of those areas to receive ongoing licenses to operate (for more, refer to the Australian Communications Media Authority). The ability to stream media services has posed a challenge to this structure and so it becomes a matter for policymakers to determine how best to advance or restore order within places.

The further away audiences are from a licensed area, the patchier the transmission signal becomes for users. Of course, for newspaper reporters and those serving large cities, areas within zones can have different cultural meanings to those who live there, creating challenges and discrepancies as to where places are and how they are understood by journalists themselves. When this understanding does not align with the audiences they serve, issues of credibility and an ability to connect with audiences are at stake.

Data from our interviews conducted as part of an Australian pilot study of the mixed fortunes of local newspapers demonstrates the challenges associated with distance, economics, and understanding cultural dimensions of space. As one editor explained through what is a quite common tale in newspapers across the globe:

> Because of economic restraints, we took two small newspapers serving two very different areas and folded them under the one umbrella. It was a mistake because those communities hated each other. And they clearly resented having to share a publication.
>
> (Hess, 2017b, p. 14)

Throughout this book, we have and will continue to highlight the issues of contestation and inequality that arise at the physical and digital boundaries of news zones and territories along with those at a perceived social distance from journalists serving places. But for now, it is necessary to highlight the continued importance of zoning for journalistic practice and the challenges of defining the extent and reach of physical zones.

We begin by understanding just how hard it can be for journalists to pin down and identify the places and the boundaries which they serve. To do this, we focus on one specific arena of contested space – "Downstate Illinois" in the US – and one specific news space, ProPublica Illinois, trying to serve audiences by understanding their geographies.

56 *Demarcating news space(s) in digital news*

Identifying place: The process of place-demarcation

Just where the "Downstate" region of Illinois is located seems an unlikely contender for a news organization's biggest challenges in times of fragmentation, competition, and deadlines. But the problem of "where" this region is came to light for staffers at ProPublica Illinois during, of all places, idle conversation in a staff meeting. "One of our reporters said something maybe like, 'Yeah, I'm driving downstate this week,'" engagement reporter Logan Jaffe explained in an email, "and another person said something like, 'Yeah, I've heard some people are kind of offended by that word.'"

ProPublica Illinois, part of the larger ProPublica news nonprofit, covers issues related to the entire state of Illinois – all 57,915 square miles of it – yet it is based in Chicago, tucked against Lake Michigan in the state's Northeastern corner. When staff members reported on news from the rest of the state, they found they possibly weren't right about where parts of Illinois were located, particularly "Downstate."

After that "watercooler" conversation, Jaffe took to Facebook in late 2017 where she put out a call asking readers to demarcate that part of the state since, in fact, the reporters had been reporting on that part of Illinois and wanted to make sure they were getting the location's borders right. Jaffe also posted to Facebook an article from the ProPublica Illinois website in which she described how she wanted to understand what she called "self-defined regionalism" as a way to articulate just how people thought the state was carved up geographically.

As an example of what she wanted to know more about, Jaffe (2017) included in her article a Wikipedia definition of "Downstate," which states the region "is all of Illinois south of the Chicago Metropolitan area." She explained in her writing online the complications of that single definition:

> It's one thing to go off of official regional boundaries – things defined by the Illinois Department of Transportation, or lawmakers – but those lines don't always align with how people feel about where they live and what they *want* to call themselves as to where they're from.

And sure enough, Jaffe quickly found a distinct disconnect between how users define – and discuss – "Downstate" issues and people in responses from social media. One Facebook user identified the region this way:

> You've probably got "Metro St. Louis," "Rural Upstate" who would still be influenced by Chicago/Milwaukee while still being farmer-rural, "University towns" (excepting CU [Champaign-Urbana] because

Demarcating news space(s) in digital news 57

it is one of the most diverse places in Illinois), "CU," "Rural southern Illinois" influenced by Nashville/Louisville/St Louis while still being a little more forest-rural, central Illinois [*sic*] influenced by Indy/Chicago/ St. Louis while still being farmer-rural, Metro-Chicago, "Quad Cities," and "Peoria."

You'll do better to be specific, since they're all pretty different culturally.

Other users also chimed in:

- "Basically, [Downstate is] anything south of I80. But usually I only hear people from Chicago use that term. I say I'm from Central Illinois. Others say Southern or West Central or East Central or Northern Illinois."
- "Downstate is a way Chicagoans try to minimize us; in my case, my house is exactly due west from the Loop. Not exactly 'down' geographically."
- "If anything, [the term Downstate is] divisive. Very us vs. them. And it's unfair and inaccurate to lump everyone not in Chicago metro with each other."

In an email interview, Jaffe said that these initial responses surprised reporters, half of whom she estimated were, like herself, not originally from Illinois. "The use of that word holds connotations for some people, and it had political and social weight to be using it, I've been learning," Jaffe said. "It's important to pay attention to how certain words rub people, because the words you choose as a reporter also say something about *you* and your life experience, too" (emphasis in original).

For us, this exchange highlights the doxic urban-rural divide that could influence readers' perceptions of state news media, much of which is based in Chicago. Furthermore, it is evidence that even in a digital age, journalism is challenged with the basics of the job – understanding where something is, who lives there, and what the place means. And, moreover, this process in fact showed how asking where a place "was" became more about what the place-name meant, a process of characterization that is discussed further below in this chapter.

Here, however, the example of "Downstate" reveals the importance and complexities of place-names absent of digital interventions and innovations that focus on the paradox of needing to understand what a geography might mean in place-name and in interpretation while also asking to locate it. The history of Illinois and the geographic distribution of power and social capital, therefore, was critical to how journalists were expected to describe (and locate and identify) regions of the state.

58 *Demarcating news space(s) in digital news*

As a point of background, while the state's capital of Springfield is set in the geographic middle of Illinois, Chicago remains the center of popular and political culture. It is imbued with cultural, political, and economic capital – the home to former US President Barack Obama, decades of local political rule by the "The Boss" Richard Daley and his son, and related financial and legal scandals that make The Windy City a space of centralized power. Chicago is also a hub of international attention, home to television sitcoms and dramas – and to news production.

The *Chicago Tribune* and *Sun-Times* dominate the legacy market, while national television channel WGN pumps out local news and syndicated entertainment to the nation. Chicago was also once the location of Oprah Winfrey's HARPO mega-entertainment site before moving to West Hollywood in 2015.

Today, US President Donald Trump's building boasts his name in gold, stories-tall capital letters on the bottom of a skyscraper on Michigan Avenue, lording over the Chicago River, directly across the street from the Tribune Tower, where the *Tribune* and WGN – as well as other media – are located. The massive Trump structure is on the site of the former *Chicago Sun-Times* newspaper building. This has long been the cluster of symbolic power in geographic space.

Yet, in 2017, the *Tribune* announced it, too, is moving from its legendary spot to a space a few blocks South, leading to an interesting court case about whether the newspaper will take its sign with it – or leave it to remind people of its nearby existence. (Name-changing is important for Chicagoans who had to deal with change of the Sears Tower to the Willis Tower a decade earlier).

But the *Tribune*'s move – and the future of the sign, which the new owners wished to keep to beautify what will become a building of condos – led to one of the newspaper's columnists to plead for the sign to remain "as a reminder of what built it" (Schmich, 2018). The columnist also reminisced about the building and its meanings, discussing what an editor from another newspaper told her earlier in her career when she was choosing whether to work for the *Tribune*:

> He leaned back in his chair, crossed his arms and assured me my fate was sealed. "You're going to walk up that Michigan Avenue," he said, "you're going to see that Tribune Tower and you're going to think, 'I am somewhere.'"

And in a strange exchange of ideas within her column, the writer highlights the desirability of "somewhere":

Demarcating news space(s) in digital news 59

On Thursday, Chance the Rapper, tweeted, "Is it (expletive) up that I wanna condo in tribune tower?"

No, Chance, it's not. The Tower is Somewhere. It will make you feel your city in a special way.

Still, with all of the media attention to Chicago – much of which is drawn from public imaginations of "city life," well established in novels, such as Dreiser's *Sister Carrie*, Midwestern grit and a splash of glam – it's not surprising that people who live in and around the metro area, or even far away in "Downstate," have to compete with the notions of cultural and social importance.

Understanding these dynamics, however, can be an added layer for journalists with various levels of familiarity with the region trying to get the news out from all around the state. "I think being from here and not from here have advantages and disadvantages," Jaffe said. She continued:

People not from here may have fresher eyes and can see different sort of narratives about a place. While, people from here have that historical knowledge about how things came to be how they are, from how they've experienced it and kept up with it. That's both an asset and a drawback.

The point we make here is that newer perspectives of places – the ability to see things differently, is a key component of the imaginative power of place. It requires a much greater and concerted effort from those with in-depth knowledge of the places they serve to try to see things that may appear most obvious in a different light, which is exactly the aim of a book such as this.

The role of distance in journalistic place-making

Throughout the rest of this we will continue to unpack the changing relationship between news and proximity that influences how journalists – digitally and otherwise – relay meanings of geography to audiences. In this section, we focus on one key aspect of distance – physical remoteness.

On one hand, physical distance between the central site of news production and those at the fringes of the news zone, or further, affect the way a story receives coverage. Journalists might be slow to arrive at breaking news, for example, or they may also miss some pertinent or nuanced meanings of geography not having spent much time in these spaces that are away from their offices and homes. Some of this distance can be represented through a lack of sources to speak to an area's issue to relying on second-hand reporting to buttress their own.

60 *Demarcating news space(s) in digital news*

Consider this comment from an Australian journalist interviewed for our research in 2013 as part of a doctoral study in Australia in terms of the demarcation of spaces into zones of journalistic productivity:

> We have a 100 kilomometre radius in terms of how far we can drive to cover a story or send a photographer because that's all time will allow us to cover when we have to travel to interview sources. And time is money.

Of course, physical distance can be overcome with forms of capital and digital technology within news zones – even with the use of journalistic stringers, frequently those who, on a freelance basis, can help to extend a news outlet's reach. Those located at the physical periphery of a news zone for example can counter-act physical distance via practices of participatory and citizen journalism.

Such "participatory" practices, however, have been explained as exploitation of free labor (Hesmondhalgh and Baker, 2001), and also as a mere furthering of journalistic norms and interpretations, as editors and reporters maintain specific standards on language, sourcing, evidence, and explanation. That said, without this cultural capital, those at the periphery may simply miss out on coverage altogether, which is a fear for those without news services in the UK (Williams, Harte, and Turner, 2014) and in other, large geographically dispersed places, such as Australia and the US. (This is not to mention the challenges of those in other nations of less popular desirability and exclusion, where journalists rarely travel and which journalism scholarship also frequently ignores.)

Still, as our research suggests, those stories that are "physically" witnessed or covered by journalists are perceived to generate more legitimacy, which we will discuss in Chapter 5, and that is a problem of equality and even journalistic accuracy in and of itself. As one Australian news user commented in an interview in October 2017:

> You can get attention in Facebook or send a photo into the newspaper, but it's far better when a journalist comes and takes your photo. It just seems more meaningful. By better I mean that it matters more.
>
> (Hess, 2017b, p. 19)

Distance need not be a continent for journalists to want and need clarification of what a space is or means. Above, we discussed the process of journalists in Illinois who wished to understand and describe where a location was, which in the end seemed to be a process of "what" a space was. Here, we again show the complexities within the process of characterizing space through the process of locating it.

Characterizing place in the news

The characterization of spaces is a mixture of processes by which journalists identify and align the meanings of geography with cultural geography – in effect attribute meaning that makes place. Natalie Pate, a reporter at Gannett's *Statesman Journal* in Salem, Oregon, tells a story of how her newspaper comes to identify and explain the geographic locations of spaces in her coverage area – as well as how that process informs the newspapers' explanations of the social conditions there.

Pate first became familiar with the Northwestern US as an undergraduate at Willamette University in Salem. Labeled by the university as the first institution of higher education West of the Mississippi River, it harks back to its establishment by religious settlers to the city that also became the state's capital. The city was built around the university. Pate refers to Downtown near the university as being at the area's "heart." Directional areas of the city emerged from the center out and are held to by journalists, officials, and citizens still today.

The *Statesman Journal* is a mid-sized paper with a newsroom of between 20 and 30, including reporters, photographers, and editors. With that staff, the newspaper – which, like other Gannett newspapers, holds the mantra of being "Part of the USA Today Network" – covers state government, education, and local news specific to "where our readership is" particularly in Marion and Polk Counties, Pate said.

The newspaper covers the Western portion of Salem, West Salem, separated from the rest of the town by the Willamette River. West Salem used to be its own town and is incorporated by Polk County, whereas the rest of Salem is in Marion County. And it's here where the national affiliation, state connections, and local geographic distinctions become complicated by named spaces – and the meanings associated with them.

To begin with, to say that something is happening in North Salem would not include happenings North of West Salem, which borders Salem West of the Willamette River. In fact, "West Salem" doesn't really have a "North Side," Pate said. Instead, saying something is North simply means that it is North of Salem's State Street – but not the entire State Street, which stretches from the river to Interstate 5. North (at least in terms of how the newspaper will define it) is generally North of the street segment that connects the university and the state capitol building.

There are also other defined geographies:

- East Salem (not a city, but the section of Salem) begins at the train tracks at 12th Street, as well as Capitol and Portland Roads – actually the same roads, but with different names as one drives North

62   *Demarcating news space(s) in digital news*

- West Salem is all west of the Willamette River
- State Street, again, is used to determine boundaries for North Salem and South Salem. Today's South Salem High School used to be Salem High School – a vital landmark for wayfinding – but which changed its name as populations moved North
- Easterly divides, in conjunction with the North-South boundary, create Northeast Salem
- The nearby community of Keizer – which the residents of Keizer divide into geographic sections – is only referred to by the *Statesman Journal* as Keizer

A map defining – or reifying – these geographies once hung in the newspaper's old offices when it was located Downtown, though it hasn't yet been replaced since the newspaper moved to South Salem in June 2017. Pate, who covers education, said she finds the geographic boundaries and characterizations appearing in many of her articles – and in discussions with the public about social conditions and their influence on policy.

"What's particularly interesting with this [geographic] breakdown," Pate said, "is that the areas are not entirely, but overwhelming have certain sections in the community where the more affluent white communities are and the low-income, minority communities are." The Northeast is overwhelmingly low income and Hispanic and more commercialized, Pate said, while the Downtown is home to cute boutiques, including on a main street, which hosts a mall and historic buildings.

As with many geographies and political boundaries, such as voting districts, official neighborhoods and tax districts shape the spaces of the overall city, but the characterizations of who lives in or who frequents these spaces hold great influence over public perceptions of space. Near Lancaster Drive in Northeast Salem, for instance, past the state mental hospital, one neighborhood was once home to what residents called "halfway houses."

Now, the space has been assigned a popular name that reflects dominant views of the geography – "Felony Flats," Pate said. Among some reporters and officials, when crime news appears there, passing jokes about the "how" and "why" include, "Oh, well that's over in Lancaster. No one lives there on purpose."

But this is where Pate lives. Historically viewed as a space for gangs and drugs in the schools in the 1990s, the schools today that serve this neighborhood are overcrowded and the conversations of the neighborhood's conditions or "negative news" from the neighborhood focus on causes related to the types of people perceived to be living there. "You can't have a conversation about anything without seeing that they are treated differently," Pate said.

Demarcating news space(s) in digital news 63

Within this dynamic of neighborhood meanings, school demographics, and nostalgia of what the neighborhood once was, it is not uncommon for the newspaper to place crime news that occurs nearby within a phrase similar to the crime having happened in the neighborhood itself. "X number of blocks near McKay High School," Pate said, is a sign that indicates the meanings of the school and what families send their children there are aligned with the crime – and the criminals. Pate notes that since this trend in coverage was brought to their attention, they have changed their ways of reporting.

However, in more white neighborhoods, Pate said, she hasn't seen coverage putting the crime near schools in the same way. And while the newspaper wouldn't refer to a geography as "Felony Flats," for instance, Pate wonders how place-names, such as "South Salem" or "Northeast Salem" may influence readers in terms of characterizing the spaces as "good" or "bad."

Pate said she's also seen how her own reporting on K–12 education in the city has disproportionally focused on more "negative" stories of schools and neighborhoods in one side of the city over another. This means the reinforcement of doxic attitudes are played out in specific geographic spaces, a result of several influences of audience expectations, political messages released to the press by civic leaders, and reports from state officials, police, and even citizens about the goings-on there.

Salem's school district holds more than 60 schools and some 42,000 students, Pate said, and when reporting about racial inequalities, funding disparities, or overcrowding, some schools appear more underserved than others. Still, she wonders about how she might be contributing to community spatial stereotypes by covering what is told to her to be news.

"I need to check myself and make sure I'm not just writing about schools in West Salem or in South Salem," Pate said. "But there is also an equity topic that disproportionately effects certain schools," leading her to cover some schools more than others if dealing with funding, dropout rates, or other issues. She said what's harder to do in these situations, though, is to express the pressures placed on the schools and the neighborhoods and students – the causes can be diverse and unwelcoming to the general community – than just stating the problems and proposed solutions.

More recently, the newspaper made steps to deal with stereotypes in covering parts of the city that often are depicted with criminal suspects arrested and booked in the local jail – editors (like many local news editors across the country in the mid-2010s) decided to remove the newspaper's infamous mugshot gallery. "That told me we were more concerned with how our coverage impacted the community than getting the clicks," Pate said.

64 *Demarcating news space(s) in digital news*

We spent this time focusing on the specifics of place-making in Salem, Oregon, because very rarely do scholars receive such detailed information about place-making that identifies the complexities of how local geographies are formed. Pate's comments highlight the nuances of place that are exposed when she is encouraged to be reflexive about her daily journalistic practices.

Questions that come from these stories of place-making that are relevant for both journalists and scholars include: "How might perceptions of certain areas within one's zone change if she is much more conscious of these representations?" and "How does the journalist herself imagine what these areas are or might become as her coverage changes?" We suspect that based on answers to these questions, news coverage would change a great deal and that the work of journalists and journalism scholars can be influential in making change. But these changes are not without work on journalistic culture and normative practice.

Interpreting geography through audience expectations

In the previous chapter, we unpacked notions of space and place to build a trichotomy of space place and territory that helps to situate a critical approach to the geographies of journalism. But it is worth spending time here to complicate the rise of a key geographic concept for journalism that also influences the demarcation of space and the characterization of place – that of mobility.

Journalists – and the institution of journalism – rely on audiences for legitimacy and to maintain authority in providing a business and service of information. Subscription numbers, ratings, and people in seats have long been ways of measuring a media outlet's success. But the involvement of audiences in the continuation of journalism has extended beyond determining what is popular and the act of paying for it. In other words, commercial journalism may be made akin to a public service, but it still produces what its purchasers want.

How journalists relay their legitimacy to audiences is, in large part, in presenting a case for legitimate relationships between audiences and the news outlet. In other words, journalists must not just interpret correctly that they are authorities of information and that audiences are reliable, engaged, and willing to participate in a producer-user performance with reporters and news product. Journalists have to ensure that the news product itself meets with geographic interpretations shared by audience members; users and producers have to appear to "be" in the same "space," as it were.

In Tulsa, Oklahoma, for instance, *Tulsa World* reporter Michael Overall identified the challenge of meeting audience expectations of geography when he discussed how the definition of his city's Downtown is a definition

Demarcating news space(s) in digital news 65

in constant flux, in large part, because of constant economic and business development. Tulsa's geography, Overall said, remains defined by a highway system that loops around the city center. "Anything inside that loop is called Downtown," Overall said. And if it's not, then it's not Downtown.

A river also divides the city, but both built and natural environments merely inform interpretation, along with the other elements of life – such as economic development (gentrification) and the mobility of individuals and collectives in and around the region. "In Tulsa, the 'parts of town' are mostly defined by the major highways and the Arkansas River," Overall summarized an email. "Of course, it's all just social convention. There's no law setting the boundaries. But the river and highways provide definite 'borders' that are widely recognized."

North Tulsa, for instance, defined by Interstate 244, reveals some "sensitivity" among the public, as the space home to a majority white population is becoming more diverse with the increase of non-whites living there. The diversification, which by some is unwelcome, has come to be represented in the term North Tulsa. "I think our readers very well understand" what is meant by the term North Side, Overall said. "I don't hear that just in the newsroom, if you go around Tulsa and you hear people talk about where things are, there seems to be broad agreement."

Newsroom editors are a bit pickier about how one defines Downtown, however, with real estate developers targeting regions in this area and wanting to influence how the "community" defines particular areas. In fact, *The World* in 2015 posted its definitions of the sides of the city on its website, and one *World* writer, Ginnie Graham (2015), wrote about an "identity crisis" of the city's neighborhoods when the map first appeared.[2]

In her piece, Graham wrote about the process of defining the city spaces:

> To get to an agreement, Realtors were consulted, zoning maps were reviewed and editors drove neighborhood streets. It was a hard-fought battle, and makes me respect the work of those drawing political or municipal boundaries.
>
> Some Realtors chuckled when we posed the questions to them. Some wouldn't give an answer, showing wisdom in recognizing a hot-button issue.
>
> As the city's population has shifted farther south, "midtown" has grown with it. The west boundary for the start of "east Tulsa" was the other sticking point.
>
> "We've had this argument in the real estate world," said Mike Craddock, president of the Greater Tulsa Association of Realtors. "A lot of it depends on how long you've been in Tulsa."

66 *Demarcating news space(s) in digital news*

Here we see a reflective (though not reflexive) process by journalists to create place and to share the outcomes of it digitally with audiences. Still, and as Overall's comments reveal, there are deeper issues of geographic and social divide that clearly remain between professional communicators and their "communities," but that are likely in the minds of how audiences expect their city to be described.

Conclusion

In this chapter, we have gone behind the scenes of news production related to geographic demarcation to reveal the detailed complexities inherent in identifying, creating, and maintaining spaces. Sides of towns, cities, and regions with directional names, generally, become normalized through orientation to geographies, institutions, and social standardizations of demographics, public policy, and wayfinding. Yet, as this chapter shows, these identifications of spaces are not static, but are fluid and require a constant process of identification, challenge, and re-institutionalization.

Journalism, this chapter also shows, is not innocent in this process of establishing long-lasting spatial identities. Journalists, in collaboration with fellow social institutions, assign dominant cultural narratives of meaning about how and why spaces are identified as they are, much of the time in ways that reinforce dominant ideologies of people, perceptions of social conditions, and desires for specific definitions of community.

In the end, it is the continued practice by audiences (or perceived audiences) to purchase media or at the very least to perform among and conform to the processes of journalism in demarcating and naming in so much as the naming and demarcation supports approved expectations and explanations of place. In the next chapter, we further explore the role of audience and journalistic spatial meaning-making as digital media and users become geographically dispersed.

Notes

1 The publication, Getting the Deal Through, provides a useful comparative site of broadcast licensing arrangements in certain countries. See https://getting thedealthrough.com/area/39/jurisdiction/42/telecoms-media-2017-indonesia.
2 *Tulsa World* editors did not provide permission to republish the map; however, as of June 2018, it was posted here: www.tulsaworld.com/tulsa-map/pdf_0015ed5e-9abd-11e5-8bc8-d36dece97e7c.html.

5 Who is where?

Complicating power, proximity, and journalistic authority

US-based clothing company L.L. Bean tapped into a new market in 2017 – selling custom-made jigsaw puzzles of people's hometowns. To get one, customers simply entered a specific address and zip code for a geography of which a map would be made and cut into puzzle pieces. The final puzzle would, according to the company, "show terrain for 7.5 miles east to west and 5 miles north to south of [the] supplied address." The "home" location would be depicted by a "house-shaped puzzle piece."[1]

At first glance, the concept of a personalized, place-based jigsaw puzzle seems like an innovative way for a retail company to commercialize our connection to place. Some disgruntled customer comments on the company's website, however, reveal the complex and nebulous ways in which geography can be interpreted and defined.

One customer, wanting a map around her or his rural Pennsylvania town in the Northeastern part of the US found the product had "almost no recognizable landmarks, which took all the fun out of it" and told other customers to "[j]ust know that you won't be able to see the house you grew up in or your school, etc." Other customers told similar tales:

- "[H]alf of this puzzle was the ocean and it was all blue and the pieces were all the same color and were too much alike. It would have been better if the puzzle had more of the city shown."
- "Ordered for my son and daughter-in-law after they moved into a new home. One caveat – they live within a mile of one of the Great Lakes and quite a bit of the puzzle was blue, making it too difficult to finish. Just sayin'!"
- "The online reference map provided shows the correct location when the address is entered, yet the printed puzzle from the vendor shows the incorrect location (4 miles off)."

Not all products are perfect – especially those that promise to be customized – and the challenges some faced with their "My Hometown Puzzle" were

68   *Who is where?*

likely based on technological issues during the production process. But these comments reveal interesting patterns faced in media production-audience relationships and highlight elements that are central to understanding geographies of journalism we have unpacked so far in this book.

There is, for example, an expectation that those "customizing" our connection to places (i.e., journalists) are in close proximity to either us or to the places we want customized or can at the very least possess the cultural knowledge to represent these places in a way we know and understand cultural knowledge to represent these places in a way we know and understand.

As we have ascertained in the previous chapters, people too, seek out material objects as symbolic tokens of the places where they develop a sense of belonging. When customer expectations are not met, there is consumer discontent. Concerns over L.L. Bean's jigsaws might not result in any considerable reputational damage for the company given its modus operandi is to sell clothes, but these aspects are certainly essential for those in the business of place-making, such as news media.

In this chapter, we discuss how proximity to space and place – still an important value that drives the selection of what is considered newsworthy – is complicated in digital newswork through the geographies of journalism. The idea of "proximity" has traditionally been associated with news or events that are geographically close to readers (Mencher, 2010) and considered among a series of important news factors which overlap and are shared across news organizations.

Today, some argue that the creation of virtual proximity via technology means the concept is now a paradox (Huxford, 2007), while others such as Shoemaker, Lee, Gang, and Cohen (2007) suggest that proximity encompasses both physical and psychological aspects for journalism practice where reporters can enhance an event's psychological closeness to overcome the negative force of long physical distance.

In the sections that follow, we extend the work that engages with the concept of proximity in a digital media environment. Ahva and Pantti (2014), for instance, outline 11 forms of proximity as they relate to journalism, which include:

- geographical
- temporal
- cultural
- emotional
- moral
- virtual
- constructed
- social-ideological

Who is where? 69

- temporal
- physical
- spatial

More recently, there has been a shift toward reemphasizing the significance of reporting and producing stories in the physical locations where news breaks, positioning the place and space discussion to more "solid ground." Oppegaard and Rabby (2016), for instance, highlight the resurgence of "place-based" news in discussions about proximity and journalism when they write:

> Historically, journalism was founded upon the interests of people to nearby events, happening in specific places . . . place-based journalism returns to those core traditions while also taking advantage of the affordances of mobile technologies to tailor experiences based on context.
> (p. 635)

Both of these research frameworks afforded by Oppegaard and Rabby and Ahva and Pantti are comprehensive and complementary to studies related to the geographies of journalism, so there is no need to reinvent the wheel here. We do contend, however, that existing scholarship on news proximity tends to bypass two of the most important dimensions of them all – proximity as power and proximity to power in changing physical and digital contexts.

In this chapter, we pay particular attention to what we term "performative proximity," that which reinforces media power in places of meaning in the digital age by constructing collectives of the powerful elites to explain everyday life. We may even extend in certain circumstances the performative nature of proximity to those who "are not there" in ways by which sources extend their power of positionality, social role, or prominence and believability to explain what a place "could be" or "most certainly is," the individual's social position taking the place of "being there."

In discussing proximity, we also extend upon three other elements of Ahva and Pantti's typology – socio-ideological proximity, temporal proximity, and the way audiences perceive journalistic proximity to places. We then shift toward assessing the relationship between proximity and notions of cosmopolitanism and paternalism in assessing "where" a story is covered and what the place at the center of the story means to audiences.

Social-ideological proximity

There is an abundance of information available in online spaces about our world and our lives, and yet not every comment or source can be illuminated

70 Who is where?

or rubber stamped as "news" by professional journalists. As Ahva and Pantti (2014) highlight, journalists' proximity to others in social space plays an increasingly important role in understanding the news process.

In order to decipher "what makes news," we should always critically engage with issues of "where" and "to whom" journalists go to find stories and why in a given context. Ahva and Pantti argue journalists shape the news and engage with audiences and sources based on those who are "close to them" in terms of social and cultural values. And, they draw on sociologist Herbert Gans, for instance, to highlight how people with similar social backgrounds to journalists are more likely to contact newsrooms as sources than individuals with different social backgrounds.

Journalists are, of course, encouraged to venture into areas where they feel "out of place" in order to shed light on important or complex social or political issues. In locations considered "foreign" or "international," for example, reporters engage the help of fixers, which we discuss later, to bridge social and cultural distances between themselves and sources of news to support their work. But not all of the problems related to proximity require an international component. Something that is considered "away" can, in fact, be close to home.

People experiencing homelessness and perceptions of "no sense of place"

Our attention here is on the struggles of those who are located within the same physical locale as journalists but are themselves separated by immense social and/or cultural distance. While increasing attention is paid to issues of cultural diversity and media reporting, consider the plight of the homeless in advanced Western societies who are subjected to intense symbolic violence because of their physical "placelessness" and social distance from the powerful and those reporting the news (Schneider, 2012).

For most of us, our "sense of place" in the world is often symbolized, in part, by the houses, apartments, or dwellings we call "home." Bourdieu (2005), for example, highlights there is perhaps no better illustration than the real estate market to highlight the interplay between forms of symbolic, cultural, and economic capital, and the reinforcement of the neo-liberal doxa that tends to favor free-market capitalism.

Those living in homelessness are at extreme social and cultural distance from dominant understandings of what it means to "live" in place. For the homeless, their "sense of place" becomes intertwined with public space (park benches, sidewalks) upon which they are perceived as unwanted intruders, while significant amounts of those legally deemed "homeless"

Who is where? 71

are, in fact, living with friends and families other than their own, but are not in spaces for which they are sole or major dwellers. Their presence either in terms of what is popularly defined as homeless or does not otherwise align with the "imagined" idea we create for such spaces or ourselves in society is left outside of dominant forms of explanation, in turn leading to stereotypes of a segment of society.

When an issue such as homelessness is perceived to be at such an immense social or cultural distance from a mainstream audience, it is often assessed against powerful doxic ideas that are negotiated and re-negotiated by those with the place-making authority to do so in a given context. Our "sense of place" – or lack thereof – means that we either align with these dominant perceptions, challenge them, or ignore them.

To illustrate this, we begin by highlighting a 2018 news article published by *The Tampa Bay Times* in Tampa, Florida, with the headline "To give or not to give: Should you hand over a dollar to a person on a street Carlson?" (Carlton, 2018). In journalistic terms, the story was "balanced" in that it sought various opinions from those within the community about the issue. Yet the very practice of posing the question of whether to help a homeless person shifted emphasis from policy and welfare to issues of integrity and morality.

The story attracted 11 initial comments on the newspaper's website. Those who advocated their opinion tended to reinforce powerful doxic ideas to give weight to their own argument, especially in terms of religious and civic virtue. This generates what Ahva and Pantii (2014) refer to as moral proximity to the story, such as this comment that appeared on the article for the *Times*:

> Although Jesus and his apostles showed kindness to beggars, they did not encourage begging; though they gratefully accepted hospitality, they did not beg. Jesus told those who followed him merely to obtain bread that their concern should be, not for "the food that perishes, but for the food that remains for life everlasting." (Joh 6:26, 27) The standard among Christians was: "If anyone does not want to work, neither let him eat."
>
> –2Th 3:10–12.

And this from another:

> Absolutely give. Luke 6:31 Jesus says "And as ye would that man should do to you, do ye also to them likewise." Keep reading Luke Chapter 6 verses 32 thru 38. Guarantee you will never think twice about helping someone and not judging others.

72 *Who is where?*

Put in context, *The Tampa Bay Times* story was itself a way of generating a "local" angle to a national news story that had made headlines just days earlier. Former Vice President of the United States, Joe Biden, had been captured on camera by a passing citizen around the same time talking to a man experiencing homelessness outside a movie theater in Washington, D.C.

The story went viral on Facebook and YouTube and generated national and international media attention. News outlets reported on Biden's compassionate gesture and sought context by interviewing the man (identified as Rashid). A story by the Associated Press (2018) was titled, "What was Joe Biden talking about with homeless man?" A CNN post was titled, "Biden seen chatting it up with a homeless man in Washington" (Cole, 2018). Generally, early stories about the photograph, which went viral, did not carry answers to what the conversation was, other than to speculate about a future presidential bid by Biden.

News coverage of homelessness tends to align with proximity to power. The debate about "undesirables" in public scenes within media is frequently described through official source information rooted in demographics and traditionally socially conservative explanations of the causes of and for homelessness that lean toward blaming victims.

These positions of power via explanation are directly related to the proximity of newsworkers – ideologically and physically – to the powerful themselves (Gutsche, 2014b). Schneider (2012), for example, draws on a content and qualitative analysis of quotations from sources in Canadian newspaper items on homelessness. From that, she argues that experts dominate as sources on the issue, and while people experiencing homelessness themselves are not entirely absent from coverage, their voices are often only heard in terms of their experiences.

Ultimately, then, quotes from those considered homeless themselves promote a narrative of homelessness that marginalizes the people who experience it and contribute to their social exclusion. Indeed, physical proximity to powerful sites and agents – even brief encounters such as Biden's moment with Rashid – can or at least can aim to generate action, change, and perhaps more often than not, reinforce the status quo. Proximity to power can also reverberate across local and global communication channels.

Proximity to power

The significance of being perceived to be physically located close to agents and sites of power generates what Bourdieu (2001) might refer to as "symbolic misrecognition" – an unspoken, tacit power to influence or to decide that some things or practices are better or worthier of others. In this way, we argue that physical proximity – even in a digital era – is seen to be more legitimate in perpetuating powerful relationships and ideas than those at a physical distance.

Who is where? 73

This continues to be reinforced by the highest levels of constitutional law which ultimately affect journalism practice. Decisions around government policy in many advanced societies are only valid, for example, if members are in parliament to make them. Nevertheless, Staines (2015) suggests there continues to be issues of discrimination attached to the appearance of criminals who appear via video-link in court, even though now there are certainly technological capabilities to make decisions from a digital distance.

Journalists' symbolic power continues to be reinforced in terms of their physical proximity to those within power in the digital world. Despite his rumblings about mainstream media, US President Donald Trump continues, even if by altering through the introduction of Skype and blacklisting, the time-honored tradition of White House press briefings (of which increasingly socially conservative journalists and bloggers are allowed to ask questions) in Washington. There, too, continue to be specially designated spaces for reporters in court rooms to ensure that justice is seen to be served (Waller and Hess, 2011).

Digital journalists still benefit from the physicality of traditional brick and mortar across the US where pressrooms tend to be held within the tombs of statehouses, city halls, and county courthouses in addition to their own buildings. In Australia, meanwhile, such buildings have long been established in the central business district – which represents the center of economic power in any given town or city.

These spaces-within-spaces put journalists further in line physically and ideologically with members of other social institutions. Together, then, the legacy of the press institution and its local, historical presence, blends with the authority of the physical location – the storied spaces within geography.

Performative proximity

Boden and Molotch (1994) argue that when it comes to understanding proximity, individuals share the desire to be near others who are understood as broadly similar to oneself. Physical co-presence with people we see as "like us" is often actively sought to establish our identity. This forms the basis of what we have introduced as "performative proximity" in the digital age – instances where the powerful (agents and/or sites) are represented together in place and time to reinforce the existing social order and media power.

Performative proximity resonates with Goffman's (1959) dramaturgical observations of "front stage" behavior that highlight the importance of certain practices as being linked to social and spatial settings. Here, public performance emerges as a self-managed series of facades where the front stage establishes the proper setting, appearance, and manner for the social roles and relationships assumed by the actors. Performative proximity positions places of meaning or significance as the theater.

74 *Who is where?*

Bourdieu's (1999) concept of "site effects" is useful here in that such sites of significance can be defined as "the point in space where an agent or thing is situated, 'takes place,' exists, that is to say, either as a localization or from a relational viewpoint, as a position a rank in an order" (p. 123). Physical sites such as political buildings from the White House in the US to Parliament House in Canberra, Australia, Wall Street, or federal courts of law are obvious sites of symbolic and economic power, as is Google Search in digital space. Agents of power in these spaces perform "on stage," as well, to highlight not only their proximity to these sites but to reinforce their own legitimacy and those of others by simply being there.

There is perhaps no better example of performative proximity than the continuing ritual of the press conference in a digital world, the coming together of agents of symbolic and media power to reinforce the significance of an event and those present, especially within parliamentary press galleries or press briefing rooms. In some instances, only certain media – even in a digital environment – are given access to these frontstage events, reinforcing agents of media power.

Huxford (2007) argues location and proximity are crucial to the promotion of journalistic authority, so much so that journalists will perform technological tricks to make it appear as though they are "there." Political broadcast journalists, for example, are regularly juxtaposed against a backdrop of parliamentary buildings (recreated with green screen tricks) to reinforce their legitimacy and authority in news reporting.

In fact, consider the role of the television journalist who reports a cyclone directly from the eye of the storm, adding to the performative drama and perceived professionalism and authority of the organization for "being there." Zelizer (1990), too, argues:

> By being proximate to events, journalists accomplish the first step in assuming responsibility for their stories and in reporting "what they see" in reliable and authoritative fashion. . . . By promoting their proximity, journalists can both claim authorship and establish authority for their stories.
>
> (p. 38)

It should be noted, nonetheless, that performative proximity is more than just the legitimacy that comes from "bearing witness" – it is an orchestrated moment that compresses places and people of meaning in time to reinforce power among those that are present.

Proximity to power in digital space

Little attention has been paid to proximity to power in digital spaces such as the way news stories are filtered and elevated on search engine results

Who is where? 75

pages, such as Google. When it comes to digital space, there are some nodes that shine brighter than others depending on where we stand in the world and as a result accumulate symbolic capital over time. Couldry (2000), for instance, argues that accelerated flows of information and people always involve "nodes" through which those flows pass. And, as Couldry writes, "what matters, economically and socially, is where you are in relation to those nodes" (p. 27).

Too often, in journalism studies, however, digital space has been celebrated as a democratizing force when the decentralization and autonomous production which characterizes the internet space also means an overflow of information and dissipation of power. Tang and Yang (2011) contend:

> For every issue made visible, thousands upon thousands more actually remain invisible: they receive little attention and manifest little power. The neglect of these invisible issues creates a rosy illusion that the internet distributes symbolic power to ordinary people.
>
> (p. 676)

News media players, too, are increasingly adopting locative technologies to follow news users via their smart devices in a mobile world, but the importance of this technological form of cultural capital means that, according the Pew Research Center, "even the weakest of the tech giants is in a far stronger financial and technological positon to develop these abilities than all but the largest of news organizations" (as cited in Goggin, Martin, and Dwyer, 2015, p. 43).

Performative proximity in digital space, then, cannot be as neatly aligned with Goffman's front stage or back stage binary; rather, proximity to sites of power in digital space depends on negotiations and maneuverings "off stage" in order for elite agents to reassemble, take a bow, and reinforce the status quo of dominant ideology. In March 2018, for example, Google announced that its algorithms would promote "authoritative" sources over "relevance or freshness" in search engine results.

The Australian newspaper lauded the decision as a step toward "recognizing the value of legitimate journalism and provenance on the internet" (Davidson, 2018). Another initiative would also see Google share data with what the company also considered authoritative sources (such as *The Washington Post, The Financial Times, The New York Times,* Fairfax *Media,* and *Mainichi* in Japan) to show which internet users had a propensity to pay for online journalism. What we see here is a unification and endorsement of power, both within news content itself to reinforce existing dominance in new digital territory.

Freelance journalist and former *New York Times* foreign correspondent Chris Hedges (2018) writes for *Common Dreams*, which describes itself as

76 *Who is where?*

a "last firewall independent media site against government and corporate lies." He covers the intersections of public notions of the internet and socio-political control enforced in its functions. Referring to the Google algorithm announcement, he writes:

> The iron wall is rising. It will cement into place a global system of corporate totalitarianism, one in which the old vocabulary of human rights and democracy is empty and where any form of defiance means you are an enemy of the state. This totalitarianism is being formed incrementally. It begins by silencing the demonized. It ends by silencing everyone.

Interestingly, then, is the question of when audience use of a product itself makes the user feel as though they are in close proximity to the powerful themselves, particularly since the user herself is contributing to the analytics, to the big data that is gathered, and to the consumption of the product being peddled online.

In fact, in April 2018 when Apple co-founder Steve Wozniak publically announced he would be leaving the Facebook platform as a user due to concerns about data privacy, he highlighted a notion similar to ours of proximity to power, but in ways that have not been adopted widely: "Users provide every detail of their life to Facebook," Wozniak wrote in a published email to *USA Today*. "Facebook makes a lot of advertising money off this. . . . Apple makes its money off of good products, not off of you. As they say, with Facebook, you are the product" (Ghosh, 2018).

Extending temporal proximity

Journalists have long assessed news value as not just where a story happens but when a story happens. The construct of breaking news is of course exceptionally temporal, so much so it continues to influence the organization of the spaces and places where journalism is practiced. In the digital age there are various degrees of temporal proximity that both shape and are shaped by the making of and engagement with news – what we might understand as "spontaneous," "homogenous," and the increasing perception of "autonomous temporality."

Regardless of how accurate information is, the importance of spontaneous temporal proximity to news and information continues to influence the competitive news landscape. Usher (2018b), in her study on breaking news production processes in United States metropolitan newspapers, argues that there continues to be a connection between spontaneous temporality and authority. As she contends:

Who is where? 77

Journalists use [breaking news updates] to retain their role as authoritative truth-tellers in relation to audiences, the competition and their own position in the profession. These metropolitan newspaper journalists worry that a breaking news story, while potentially necessary, is also questionable and even potentially harmful, but nonetheless pursue it.

(p. 21)

Social media has increased competition for the news story first, and a clear reaction to breaking news can indeed initiate the performative proximity ritual we outlined earlier. Benedict Anderson's emphasis on "homogenous empty time," meanwhile, positioned secular modes of thoughts as replacing transcendentality through the constructed importance of time measured by clocks and calendars. While media and technology provide the capabilities of simultaneity, homogenous empty time is now immensely uneven, and the digital environment has unraveled some media practices that many have once generated a sense of shared "imagined" social unity.

There is not scope in this book to engage in a full thesis on the relationship between news media and temporality in the digital age. Rather, in terms of temporal proximity it is important to highlight the increasing perception of autonomous temporality as it relates to journalism practices – that is the audience's ability to relegate the dominance of clock-now time and therefore begin to exercise their own meanings within experimental temporal spaces.[2]

Autonomous temporality is, simply put, a matter of having control over how one chooses to use one's own discretionary time (Goodin, Rice, Parpo, and Eriksson, 2008). There is perhaps no better illustration of the increasing value of perceived temporal autonomy to journalism than in the rise of immersive journalism. It is the most high-tech exemplar of the time-space compression in the digital world and reinforces the idea of autonomous temporality both in the way audiences are encouraged to access content at their discretion along with the relatively unlimited time users have to explore the 360-degree surroundings and virtually absorb themselves in places as presented in these virtual reality experiences.

The New York Times library of VR projects, for example, is largely constructed around stories that have both visual and narrative appeal, rather than immediate or breaking news value. Instead of generating a sense of homogenous time that reinforces the values of a collective, the emphasis is on shared time between the audience and the reporter. Consider the newspaper's promotional paragraph that leads its online VR collection:

Stand alongside Iraqi forces during a battle with ISIS. Walk on a planet three billion miles from the sun. Join our award-winning journalists

78 *Who is where?*

at the center of it all. Explore the library of 360-degree virtual reality experiences for yourself.

(*The New York Times*, 2018)

While virtual reality promotes the idea of seeing through someone else's eyes, the idea of "joining our award-winning journalists at the center of it all" reinforces the power dimensions between the audience and journalism in the digital age. Immersive journalism illustrates the power and advantage to news media in recreating the perception of being "in place" through new technological tools.

The Tow Center for Digital Journalism contends that virtual reality challenges core journalistic questions evolving from the Fourth Estate debate on "who is a journalist," what a journalist represents, and whether journalists should have a "place" in the VR experience or should serve as objective bystanders. To us, this merely highlights the vital importance of understanding journalism's relationship to place-making in the digital age.

Temporal proximity, for example, highlights the need to position not just the mobility and accessibility of news at any time, but the way news media shape understandings of places in terms of their past, present, and future (Clancy, 2014). Appreciating the generation of collective memory, too, via journalism, historical artifacts, and "imagining what" places might be in the future all form part of the temporal dimensions of place as asserted via news media.

Audience perceptions of journalistic proximity to place

Throughout this book, we have highlighted the symbiotic relationship between audience "sense of place" and the news. For example, we have touched upon how Ahva and Pantti (2014) emphasize the importance of audience proximity in terms of news outlets' understanding who their audience is and how to engage them.

Little attention, however, is paid to understanding the relationship between the ways audiences view journalists' proximity to places over time. In other words, moving beyond the idea of who is there to report a story when it happens (which we will return to shortly), to the way journalists themselves develop an appreciation and understanding of the places that matter to audiences over time.

Hess and Waller (2017), for example, develop the construct of local habitus as it applies to news media and journalism – the powerful set of dispositions and practical logic developed within a place. They argue local habitus can translate into cultural capital that is "embodied" as it evolves

Who is where? 79

from long-lasting dispositions of the mind and body and can be understood as a particular cultural competency that is sometimes acquired "quite unconsciously" (for more, see Bourdieu, 1986, pp. 244–245). Such notions of embodiment can affect a news outlet's reputation if journalists who are positioned as place-makers lack an imagined understanding of the place, from pronouncing street names "correctly" to knowing the direction that a river flows through a town.

Such embodied knowledge of places makes the reliability of geo-tagging technology and software difficult to establish in local settings. Cai and Tian (2016) found that place references in local news have their special vocabulary and that their ambiguities are handled differently by local people who have direct experiences with those places. Their study showed there to be a significant portion of place-names in local news that are vernacular, are vague places, or of finer granularity than those found in gazettes in gazetteers and atlases, highlighting the subtleties that shape the symbolic and imaginative importance of place to news users.

Hess and Waller (2014) contend that the depth and quality of a journalist's knowledge of environmental, social, and economic features of the place have important economic and cultural value for the news outlets they represent. It goes to the trustworthiness and legitimacy of the news they produce, affecting sources' and readers' decisions about providing news and buying it. Yet, threats to journalistic proximity to place (and ultimately reputation) are perhaps most evident in small-town media which is increasingly subjected to the centralization and dispersion of news resources (Hess and Waller, 2017).

Here, journalists are often relocated to larger metropolitan news hubs, reporting or producing stories from a distance or being parachuted into towns when and if they are required without developing a "feel for place." It is also here where we see a return to the importance of the degrees of place-making that happen depending on the geographic location of a reporter. This is not to say, however, that journalists are any better at "knowing" their cities and boroughs, focusing on official sources and stories and relying on dominant, stereotypical explanations of social conditions and populations to "cover" inner-cities (Shumow and Gutsche, 2016).

Physical proximity: From cosmopolitanism to rituals and vigils in reporting the "where" of news

Proximity and the notion of cosmopolitanism have been used to frame the moral relationship between the Western viewer and the distant sufferer. Silverstone (2007), for instance, positions cosmopolitanism as the orientation

80 *Who is where?*

of openness toward distant others, which relies on technological mediation to raise the moral imperative to act on those others in the name of common humanity. Additionally, Kogen (2017) writes about how journalists explain the coverage of what Boltanski (1999) refers to as "distant sufferers."

Journalism students are frequently introduced to the images of a vulture lording over a starving child as a means by which to discuss ethics (and morals) of covering the news that is perhaps unfamiliar, the "foreignness" of it potentially influencing how and why journalists should take the picture, help the starving child, or come up with additional actions. Questions that generally emerge in such discussions include, "Do journalists intervene?," "Is such an image acceptable for publication?" Rarely do journalists ask, "Why are we here?" and "What do we do with the news we produce because we are here?" Instead, some newsrooms simply employ the "breakfast test," asking "Will audiences be comfortable with this while eating breakfast?" (Shapley, 2013).

Professional ideology of journalists covering the world from afar mandates that questions be asked about the financial, political, and social issues inherent in the reporting, but little work later by journalists offers rigorous self-assessment of the us/them dichotomy found in covering even-banal news events and items from a sense of Western "medianess" (Goss, 2015). One of the questions journalists should be asking in making decisions about covering "there" from "here" (even if the journalist herself is "there") include: "What if this was happening in my backyard?"

In covering places of "there," Kogen (2017) acknowledges interactions of conflict, drama, and human interest storytelling deemed necessary to many journalists to engage audiences with journalistic product, which is an additional level of justification journalists use to cover what they do and how they do it, particularly in "international" news. More specifically, journalists reported to Kogen that in covering issues of starvation or other humanitarian challenges "abroad" they struggle with finding a balance between providing information about an international crisis, and keeping audiences interested in news that happens somewhere else.

International journalists, meanwhile, have long used "the fixer" to become introduced or acclimated to unfamiliar geographies, cultures, language, and communities as a way to get to the news, but also as a way to find voices of the communities being covered from elsewhere – and by people from elsewhere. Fixers, who are frequently paid to take journalists into dangerous areas of news coverage during times of war or crisis, are expected not only to be aware of the socio-political elements of conflict, but to prepare journalists to present complicated information accurately dissected and

Who is where? 81

explained. (Note, the fixer process is also used by global militaries, as some governments – including the US – also turn to academic scholars in similar ways to wage war.)

Yet, a recent study of the journalist-fixer relationship by the Global Reporting Center reported distinct differences in how fixers and reporters operate, are treated as professionals, and present information (or desire to present information) to audiences. Among their findings, as reported by Neiman Reports, are the following (Klein and Plaut, 2017):

- More than 70 percent of journalists stated they rarely, if ever, asked fixers to operate in situations of immediate danger; 56 percent of fixers said they are "often" or "always" placed in danger to assist journalists
- 44 percent of journalists reported being questioned by fixers about the editorial focus of a particular project; 80 percent of fixers said they have questioned journalists' focus
- 50 percent of journalists say fixers have corrected their understanding or presentation of information; 80 percent of fixers report correcting journalists' interpretations

Such a survey, without doubt, is ripe with limitations and challenges, and cross-cultural communication – let alone international journalism – is rich because of its subjectivities and the challenges inherent in understanding one another. Yet, interpretation of knowledge is vital to the role of both the journalist and the fixer – as is the way journalists and their agents are treated, particularly during high-stress stories and in relationships in which the journalists are almost always paid better, receive credit for their reporting, and have ultimate authority in what (and how) information from the field is presented to audiences.

Yet, the fixer-journalist relationship reveals the intricacies of reporting in some place one is not from. Research has long tracked where journalists live and where they report, finding geographic divides within the communities where journalists cover the news. The fixer relationship may seem, on the surface, to be so unique that it cannot be applied to understanding source relationships elsewhere, yet journalists – even in their own geographies – turn to similar forms of knowledge-gathering to understand spaces and stories that might be unfamiliar.

Research clearly indicates the dangers of unfamiliarity of geography and place experiences (Derickson, 2017). Lauren McGaughy (2017), a reporter with the *Dallas Morning News*, wrote for her newspaper an open apology to Sutherland Springs, Texas, a small-town that suffered a mass shooting in November 2017 and that suffered again with an onslaught of journalists

82 *Who is where?*

to cover the killing of 26 people. McGaughy – who was among the initial reporters to "parachute" into the city and was as unfamiliar as many other reporters with the town, its people, and its culture – writes that from her experience "there *must* be" a "better way to cover a tragedy like this."

McGaughy's open letter depicts a town "without so much as a stoplight" in a nostalgic fashion of "small-town pastoralism" (Gans, 2004) that emerges from so many during journalistic reflections upon intrusive behaviors during times of covering crisis. McGaughy's note marks the space as being plagued by a "scrum engulfing your friends and loved ones, photographers, and reporters with iPhones jockeying to capture an image" of neighbors sobbing, hugging, lighting vigil candles "that didn't also include the media melee."

And though McGaughy recognizes that she, herself, was welcomed into victim's homes and got her "scoop," she notes that the interactions of journalists from elsewhere (in fact, almost all of the reporters were new to the town) were less than acceptable even though the story was justified for coverage because of the number killed.

Such a focus on getting the story from a place – a country, city neighborhoods, or country hamlet – is based on the degree to which journalists believe audiences will find the story interesting. But the interest is not only in the context of the story – the number killed, the economic impact of development, the political scandal or sensation. The interest is two-fold: Where the story is and what journalists think audiences will think of it plays a role in news coverage, as well.

A school shooting in Parkland, Florida, outside of Miami in 2018, for instance, was treated in national media as a suburban story, in which the survivors led to international protests against gun violence. In this case, the story spread from a wealthy suburb to city centers across the world where citizens with disposable incomes led the march (though students from all walks of life chose to leave school in protest, as well).

There were also racialized connotations of this suburban shooting. Though the Parkland shooting involved students from a variety of racial groups, the story was based in a largely white and Latino part of South Florida while scores of "black-on-black" or "gang" violence occurs across the country and is treated, largely, as fodder for suburban imaginations of inner-city decay and violence (Yanich, 2005).

Additional voices appeared later in 2018 as black students at Parkland expressed concern and disappointment that non-black students led the charge without them to attack gun violence, ultimately ending up on the cover of *Time* while at the same time, non-black students went to other parts of the country – into the black urban inner-cities – to discuss the same kind of gun violence plaguing black neighborhoods across South Florida (Ruiz-Grossman, 2018).

Who is where? 83

Historically, however, physical and ideological violence in black communities has been seen as a problem of specific US cities – Chicago, New York, Los Angeles – and ignored or diminished in spaces not highlighted in entertainment and news media, including rural and suburban spots and spaces (English, 2011).

Questions remain in discussions of how journalism rituals are changing in covering place, at least in terms of the critical and cultural practices of selecting spaces to cover that represent dominant ideological narratives of meaning. What becomes another question, perhaps is how the role of audiences (who and what journalists believe audiences to be) might also be part of the problem that needs addressing in understanding how and why journalists create news.

Conclusion

In this chapter, we have outlined the potential problems and theoretical solutions related to interactions of audience, proximity, and digital journalism. Proximity in a digital age is frequently presented as a challenge that is easily addressed via metrics, comments, and social media profiles that are visible to the professional producers.

However, as we have shown here, we may not know what we think we do about our users and audiences, particularly in terms of how we (and they) relate to geographies of journalism. The imagined audience (Thrift, 2007) and where those people are will remain a constant challenge for journalists in terms of providing evidence by which they can conduct reflexive actions about how and what they publish.

In the next chapter, we discuss the spatial dialectic of place-making in journalism that leads to maintenance and further creation of social inequalities based not only on the stories that journalists tell about people but also on places.

Notes

1 As of April 2018, the company no longer provided a URL for the product, nor were reviewer comments available online.
2 We stop short of suggesting that people can access news "anytime anywhere" – that is a fallacy that masks understanding time as a human construct that exists to facilitate a degree of social order, binaries between work/leisure but which also depends on physical geographic factors such as the difference between night and day and, therefore, by default limit the window of opportunity in which we can access the news.

6 Power, place, and the spatial dialectic of digital journalism

In January 2017, US President Donald Trump, in a closed-door meeting, said that he just couldn't understand why the US should extend protections for immigrants, particularly those from "shithole countries" (Scott, 2018). Namely, journalists suggested in coverage about Trump's comments that these countries included Haiti, countries within Africa, and, given campaign-era comments from Trump about immigration and economy, Mexico.

Many questions would have to be asked to know why Trump would consider these to be "shithole countries," but there the comment was, right in the open, and journalists found themselves needing to explain the context for his statement. They also were forced to explain why a sitting president would make such a statement.[1]

It is perhaps safe to suggest that many working journalists in the US have never set foot on the soil of Trump's "shithole" nations, but that within dominant discourse about the US and "other nations," we can all "imagine" what "those places" might be like. Certainly, enough is produced in news, film, and documentaries – even in commercials for NGOs seeking money for children in developing nations – that we have a collective sense of where those places are and what they are like.

With a focus on the virtues of Edward Soja's (2010) spatial dialectic – the process of spatial power and placement of institutions and meanings within a set geography (i.e., that a hospital is placed near areas of social power and police stations near areas of danger or immense safety) – this chapter extends our thinking in previous chapters about the idea that place-making in the news can, in part, serve as ideological indoctrination to positions of power.

Through this chapter, we articulate the interactions of audiences, geography, and power to address the institutionalization of place-making within a digital atmosphere. This chapter provides an interdisciplinary analysis of press and place that functions in a critical, racial, spatial, and institutional sphere of social interactions.

Power, place, and the spatial dialectic 85

We begin by addressing a main challenge to assessing this perspective that is rooted in the demand of quantifiable (and popular) data about everyday life, our cities, towns, and nations, while also building arguments about digital journalism's collaboration with nefarious activities of today's digital world – those of surveillance and social control. "Digital distraction" (Gutsche, 2017) keeps audiences and scholars away from examining power relations of new technologies through the introduction to and of "newness."

Digital distraction: Hiding place-making in digital newswork

Movement of scholars, journalists, and audiences away from critical investigation of issues and meanings of news and its practice has occurred in recent years through the process of "digital distraction," which we define as:

> normative rhetoric that "digital media" technologies and ideologies [that] hold inherent power to evoke social change while ignoring issues of control, power, and subjugation inherent in the very rhetoric of technological development.
>
> (Gutsche, 2017, p. 363)

This distraction, Gutsche writes, is a "shield" that "halts efforts to alter media in meaningful ways and that, instead, produces the status quo of a veiled system of media control as being in and of itself a representation of slight progress" (p. 334). In other words, celebratory discussion of making journalism "better" aligns social actors away from notions of media surveillance, mass consumption, and journalistic hacking and control, and with social practice that has, in recent bouts, contributed to big data studies, the Twitterverse, and in a rise of limited methodologies to make and justify knowledge.

Distraction has also been used in regards to digital technologies more broadly, particularly in terms of how the interaction with tablets, wearables, sensors, and screens keep people from their work, from face-to-face interaction with others, and from concentrating on social issues through traditional means of communication and related actions (Green, 2018). Interestingly, though, many of these concerns come from the business sector and from places of formal education, both of which are institutions of their own indoctrination processes.

Their collective concerns are that with the introduction of digital technologies, and businesses will be torn away from using workers to make the most profit possible as they are lost in virtual worlds. Our concern with this form of "digital distraction," however, is similar only in that individuals are

86 *Power, place, and the spatial dialectic*

distracted by the flash and flair of new technology in journalism, particularly, and that one form of indoctrination – to that of journalistic meaning and interpretation of life – is in fact enhanced through passive acceptance of new ways of storytelling. Media power is reinforced through the "advanced" and "innovative" medium and enhanced through normalization and seduction.

In other words, the problem of distraction here is that individuals become separated from the source of the information and the deeper meanings inherent in the messages they consume as they are captured by technological means, design, and messages. Moreover, there is also concern within this arena of distraction that particular types of "journalistic evidence" (Gutsche, 2017) become more empowered and authoritative than others.

Qualitative and subjective voices may reign in realms of video storytelling, podcasts, and social media threads, but meaning-making in digital journalism is frequently "made" with data visualization, interactive charts and maps, hacking, and coding projects that entice citizens to the system that truly remains professionalized but which often relies on the free labor of users to create content that is sold for corporate profit.

Simanowski (2016) refers to a "seduction" of quantitative measures and a diminishing of personal interactions as though the true reason and believable facts must be (or be able to become) digital, quantifiable, and evidence-based data. This seduction of evidence via digital means (collection and measurement) and media interpretation and distribution also carries with it a sense of paternalism, particularly within the journalism that disseminated the data.

As we see it, the way we come to understand places via media continues to be based upon official forms of "journalistic evidence," which being measured by quantitative means and reinforced by "official" words of authority from fellow institutions. In terms of geography, specifically, journalists often see the world through the lens of power institutions, such as governments, business, police, and military. They may have greater access to the views of everyday citizens, but often these perspectives are outsourced (linked to) social media pages such as Facebook.[2]

In making places media, too, function to create "spaces of pain" (Thrift, 2007, p. 284), in which the space discussed and described is shown as a benchmark of acceptable undesirability, fear, and threat or suffering. These processes of indoctrinated observation via news coverage function within a landscape of official and measurable (quantifiable) forms of suffering. A space such as "The Middle East" is presented as a place-name among visuals of suicide bombing and war-torn environments while Silicon Valley is represented in mainstream media as a capitalistic commonwealth of innovation.

Power, place, and the spatial dialectic 87

Appelgren (2017) argues that not only does journalistic control in advancements of digital technologies include the selection and interpretation of information for audiences but also the means by which audiences are able to interpret data journalism through interactivity. This form of audience control, paternalism, is grounded in protecting the audience from itself, creating desirable means by which users are guided to information, informed about what to do with the information, and encouraged on how to interpret the information through visual aids, technological tools, and limitations related to the accessing, sharing, and limitations of narrative expression.

For example, an online application that was created by journalism professors at Florida International University in Miami, including one of this book's authors (Gutsche, 2015b), is an example of how users are forced into distinct narratives that, according to design and the intention of data manipulators, fail to provide deeper contexts of power relations. The Sea Level Rise App (eyesontherise.org/app) was created to help journalists and citizens in South Florida visualize the effects of rising waters.

As users entered their address to the app, they were able to locate their home and use a scrubber to change the rise of water. In many areas, six feet of rise led to a blue hue appearing and darkening the geography, suggesting that without massive changes to infrastructure, the land would succumb to sea level rise.

The application gained international attention from journalists and the scientific community, was presented at the White House, and led to university engagement with communities across the Miami region, starting in 2015. Yet, the application is also absent of context. While data from other sources indicate that the poor and racially segregated portions of the region are more susceptible to rising water, the application merely created visually appealing design for showing what could happen.

Because it was politically "safe" to ignore visualizing inequalities in a region of the country prone to boosteristic conversations about addressing sea level rise (Shumow and Gutsche, 2016) – though such an effort to alter the app was proposed at one point (eyesontherise.org/investigation) – the tool for journalists told a single story for users, one absent of discussions related to power. The result of such paternalism is not just to maintain an authority of the journalistic narrative by creating a single explanation of the data, but in the levels of legitimacy of the information source, which in this case was a research university and its journalism professors.

Safe realms of professional and scholarly critique exist, though – as they did in the case of the sea level rise application among some local journalists – through industry-wide discussions of once taboo topics of privacy and surveillance which have become the favorite topics. Replacing these as no-go topics are coded language of racism, gender, and

88 *Power, place, and the spatial dialectic*

capitalism embedded in today's journalistic algorithms, design of technological tools, and the existence of the same in the everyday banality of news (Hess and Gutsche, 2018).

As we have stated, journalists – and the institution of journalism – rely on audiences for legitimacy and to maintain authority in providing a business and service of information. That journalists have adopted social media to make it easier and more convenient for people to "follow" them has generated what might best be described as a "Pied Piper effect," where news media is awakening to the discovery that those who provide the pipe (the technology) wield increasing power.[3]

Distraction via seduction to success measures

Geographies of journalism as we have described them, become diluted by wide definitions of audience in digital journalism that are being ever-expanded and measured. Largely, the economic and symbolic value of journalism practice remains assessed by hits, clicks, views, and professional awards for the most innovative tool or technique, while others rely on industry websites and publications to legitimize and justify their existence – even if these measurements of success lack critical analysis.

In March 2018, for instance, journalism think tank NiemanLab announced that local news start-up "partner" WhereBy.Us, with the motto "Live like you live here," was doubling its local newsletters across the country. Seen as an effort to engage with citizens and communities – for some reason a measurable outcome of journalism within the digital realm – it provides news and event information targeted at "cities [that] are growing, where there are educated young people shaping and living in the urban core" (Schmidt, 2018). NiemanLab highlighted that the organization was focusing on its success with hyperlocal and fairly hipster digital publications in Portland, Oregon and Orlando, Florida, while also desiring further growth in Miami, Florida, and Seattle, Washington.

And while WhereBy.Us newsletters focus on some elements of gentrification and inequality, they largely breed stories that celebrate the cities in which they are based, or better, enhance single definitions of "community" via tales of quirky characteristics that can only really be interesting to people with disposable time and money. Stories in April 2018 from the WhereBy.Us partner in Miami, The New Tropic, for instance, featured new podcasts in the city about entertainment and economy, how people can get and stay physically fit, and events related to music, environmental film, and the start-up scene. One story focused on "women of color overlooked" in South Florida history.

Power, place, and the spatial dialectic 89

In Seattle, The Evergrey affiliated site discusses political issues related to national news media, transportation advancements in the city, and public art. Along with articles about the "4 best Seattle spots to explore on foot" and videos asking people what they think "of Seattle's rapid growth," a 3-minute video features some residents smiling and celebrating growth amid an economic boom but comments that some people might be being "pushed out of their homes" as new people move in. A jazzy piano piece plays in the background.

Despite the few instances of side comments in these posts that the cities have a history of racial and economic divide – and that those challenges still exist – the "boosteristic" (Gutsche, 2015a) fashion of this coverage resembles the move by many new media projects also celebrated by media for their "civicness" through consumption.

In turn, critical evaluations and cautions of digital technologies – and related measurements of journalism's "success" – are frequently presented within fields of practice as much as within academic circles as being that of luddites or determinists who are aiming toward dystopia. But the issues of measuring success through digital valuation of audience continues to be a problem, which enhances the desire to target particular audiences – and particular stories and particular places – in ways that privilege some over others.

In April 2018, the US-based Poynter think tank wrote about how *The Seattle Times* uses analytics to measure journalistic success (Hare, 2018). By using metrics from Google, Chartbeat, LiveFyre, and Crowdtangle – in what sounds like a scene from the streaming series *Black Mirror* – digital subscribers are assigned a level of "influence." In turn, these reports and approaches to measuring audience have shown an "influence" on what kinds of stories seem to increase subscription.

Poynter focused on the work of one real estate reporter in Seattle whose story on the influence of Amazon.com on the city's economy was recorded as attracting some 140 subscribers to the digital site. Another story, one about "tiny apartments," received 100,000 page views and led to seven new subscriptions. According to the reporter, Mike Rosenberg, the lessons learned reveal place-meanings about who the imagined – and desired audiences – are, based on geographic proximity:

> The consensus is we'd rather have a story that had a smaller number of good readers who wind up subscribing than a viral story that a bunch of people in New York and Chicago read but will never come back to Seattle again.

Interestingly, the Poynter article addresses the belief that the experiments at the *Times* somehow reveal (at least to the newspaper's vice president of

90 *Power, place, and the spatial dialectic*

innovation) that "[p]eople want local, in-depth news" and that they "care about government, accountability, and transparency" while wanting to "know how their region is changing." Yet no information is provided about what percentage of the subscribers are indeed locally based, nor was there discussion on the power of real estate to journalism, which is the heart of place for so many people and in western societies rooted in a neo-liberal doxa.

Indeed, the Poynter article also reveals another troubling element of digital journalism, highlighted by its headline, "*The Seattle Times* is making it everyone's job to grow digital subscribers" and the normalization of increased labor among "everyone" in a time when, openly, the news industry struggles with journalists having to work longer and harder with reduced job stability and prospects.

These "innovative" approaches to "doing news" are left as a legitimate measure with little critical analysis of the continued profitability of news outlets across the globe and immense pay and incentive levels for corporate leaders. Here, aspects of digital innovation distract audiences (of journalists, nonetheless) from issues of capitalism and tenets of journalism that are slighted in aims for financial profit.

This writing is not calling for a moral panic associated with "newness" within the news. Our concerns here are related to adaptation. Already, journalists alter their behaviors to use or to be influenced by digital technologies, such as in selecting what becomes news via audience analysis, evaluating the information for credibility through fact-checking software, assessing the meanings through sourcing using social media, and in selling products via push notifications.

Yet, little discussion is had about how these technological advancements influence the ideological work that journalists do. In his seminal work, *The Whale and the Reactor*, for example, Winner (1986) writes about a similar concern, which deserves to be noted here at length:

> Judgements about technology have been made on narrow grounds, paying attention to such matters as whether a new device serves a particular need, performs more efficiently than its predecessor, makes a profit, or provides a convenient service. Only later does the broader significance become clear, typically as a series of surprising "side effects," or "secondary consequences."
>
> (p. 9)

Advancements in communication have allowed us to enter self-defined filter bubbles of ideological exposure and social interaction in which we appear to be in control, but within which we are acting within realms of information created by (and for) others. In other words, we may seem to create our "Daily Me," but the selections we are provided and from which we choose to be exposed are really put there by someone else.

One must ask the degree to which journalism practice, in its most recent alterations, has adopted a greater sense of watchdogging the private citizen as they have the private corporation and the public official and agency.[4] That is a very difficult thing to measure, no doubt. But the work must begin to expand how we evaluate journalism practice as a social *and cultural* process of power, as journalism expands as a topic of dissection and debate during a rise of "fake news," for instance.

In the end, scholars, and practitioners must apply what we likely all may already know: "By changing the shape of material things," Winner (1986) writes, paraphrasing Marx, "we also change ourselves" (p. 14).

Digital surveillance and social control in journalistic place-making

When Mark Zuckerberg testified before the US Congress in April 2018 to explain Facebook's handling of user data, issues of privacy were at the forefront of the discussion. During the hearing, Senator Dick Durbin asked, "Mr. Zuckerberg, would you be comfortable sharing with us the name of the hotel you stayed in last night?" in order to highlight why Facebook users were concerned about data breaches and an invasion of privacy, especially in response to the Cambridge Analytica scandal (Balakrishnan, Salinas, and Hunter, 2018).

The digital environment brings with it a heightened era of surveillance that, for some users, occurs not as a choice but as a result of being forced into behaviors or user agreements which are standard and non-negotiable. From cookies and tracking and collection of user data to access to digital communication, digital journalism, too, uses mapping that identifies individuals' and collectives' sometimes private spaces within public spaces. Virtual reality holds the potential to go "deeper" into individuals' geographies and social collectives, and digital images via drones, cell phone cameras, and massive public datamining become published by conglomerates for public consumption, including by state and police actors.

The point is that news media are not immune from these digital data exploitation debates. As Zuckerberg faced a grilling in Congress, some of the world's biggest mastheads had just weeks earlier celebrated a deal with Google to gain access to its "Propensity to Subscribe" technology, that is

92 *Power, place, and the spatial dialectic*

Google's ability to share data that uses "signal based artificial intelligence to help publishers predict when and why a reader is likely to pay for the content on their website" (Davidson, 2018). A trial is already taking place with *The Washington Post*.

This surveillance of daily lives via online, and tracking of the "places we go" and "places where we are," has not only shaped scholarship in terms of new ways of looking at our online and physical lives through the lens of being watched (Christensen and Jansson, 2014; Gutsche, 2017), but also places journalism within a new frame of "watching" in order to control ideological meanings of the world through how – and what – we view.

The degree to which issues of social control, surveillance, and media intersect in geographies of journalism, especially social and digital geography, is perhaps strongly illustrated by China's proposed social credit system. This is being piloted in provinces across the country – and eerily similar to the "influence" project used by journalism outlets in the US, including *The Seattle Times*, as discussed above.

In China, the system is based on the government's phrase "once untrustworthy, always restricted" and gives individuals social credit ratings for their level of civic mindedness and social behavior. Surveillance and facial recognition software is used to identify details about people and vehicles. Citizens are given increased scores for donating blood or volunteering with the elderly, but a poor credit rating from being caught smoking on a train or jaywalking can mean individuals are restricted from public transport (Fullerton, 2018).

Scores are shared with others on Chinese social media and in newspapers, and so far Chinese authorities claim they have banned more than seven million people who they deem as untrustworthy from boarding flights because of a lack of social credit.

Journalists themselves are also caught up in this new form of symbolic, digital warfare given China's tight media regulation and control. A journalist who lives in China's Chonqing municipality told the Australian Broadcasting Corporation that he was "dumbstruck" to find himself banned by airlines because he was on a list of "dishonest" people after losing a defamation suite in 2015 and was asked to pay a fine, which is still outstanding (Xu and Xiao, 2018).

As part of the proposed policy, authorities in Shenzhen also recently launched the use of online shaming to crackdown on small crimes such as jaywalking. Local police launched a public website to name and shame offenders. How this effort may make its way into Chinese journalism as a normalized and legitimate form of social control – for the benefit of the masses, one would suspect the argument would go – remains to be seen.[5]

Power, place, and the spatial dialectic   93

Journalistic processes of place-shaming

In Western countries, media shaming has already been a powerful cultural practice for centuries (Waller and Hess, 2011), but as the case in China illustrates, shaming seems to be increasingly heightened – or at least appears today in powerful and overt manners – in a digital era. While anyone armed with the most basic surveillance equipment (a mobile phone, for example) and access to social media has the ability to impose shame – a practice known as souseveillance (Gutsche, 2017) – it is especially effective when reinforced or amplified by powerful arbiters of shame, such as news media (Waller and Hess, 2011).[6]

Of course, there is difficulty in examining the degree to which something is truly "right" or "wrong," yet these moral codes that fluctuate across collectives and over time operate outside of the judgement of a single moment's sensibilities. Journalism, therefore, serves within those moments not only to position social acts within an analysis of sensibilities but within an overarching, dominant ideological system of mores.

This power can be too great for some journalists to bear and yet the process and ramifications of shaming are rarely discussed in textbooks on "how to practice" journalism. One American reporter, for example, in a reflexive piece for *The Guardian*, "Why I quit: Local newspapers can needlessly ruin lives for empty clicks" (Pauli, 2017), wrote:

> As the sole crime reporter at a daily paper in Butte, Montana in charge of putting out the daily blotter, I found the process for deciding which poor residents of my city to shame completely arbitrary . . . we blow small crimes out of proportion and ruin people's lives for pennies, all while missing the big picture.

Shaming, too, comes with blaming, including what Thrift (2007) refers to as "spaces of blaming," those spaces in which depictions of the geography in media and popular rhetoric is so great that some geographies have become "zones of the world in which the circumstances are so unbearable that belief starts to fade that these circumstances will ever come to an end" (p. 286). In the US, for instance, these spaces in journalism tend to be the "ghettos" or the swaths of rural land within which "rednecks" reside. These are spaces depicted within journalism and popular media, generally, as being without hope and without possible resolution.

As with war and violence, digital worlds – from virtual reality to social media – operate to examine and describe such places "under the gaze of the media" (Thrift, 2007, p. 282) complete with scenes and evidence of social

94 *Power, place, and the spatial dialectic*

interactions, language, and dominant interpretations of acceptable behavior with which news coverage itself holds "affective form[s], bound up with the generation of emotional response" through the legitimacy and forms of journalism.

Journalism becomes important in the explanation or further exploration of public comments about places in the world in order to legitimize dominant explanations of what was said and to further build the authority of the journalistic institution as a meaning-maker. In context of Trump's comments about "shithole" countries, one conservative news commentator on CNN argued that while Trump wished to ban immigration from some nations, he had opened the doors to those from Asian regions, likely because of popular belief that these are wealthy enough or offer financial benefit to the US economy (Scott, 2018); Asian regions, apparently, are not shitholes.

But it was within comments from other nations – those titled as being a "shithole" – that identified the complications of international politics and challenges associated with geographic imaginations, particularly in terms of how we in one geography interpret and express meanings of another. On Twitter, following Trump's comments, Nana Akufo-Addo, the president of Ghana, said he was "shocked" by the characterization of his nation and wrote that "Africa and the black race deserve the respect and consideration of all" (Taylor, 2018a).

Other international leaders also spoke out about previous comments Trump had made to African officials in which he created a nation called Nambia, when surely he must have meant Namibia (Taylor, 2018b). Indeed, Trump's disdain for countries other than his own relates to conservative ideologies related to notions of race and money – measured by how many "others live there" and how much money the US supplies to a specific country in aid – which inform his perceptions, and fuel his comments – so his defenders stated.

Rev. Robert Jeffress, a Baptist pastor in Dallas, Texas, attributed to be one of Trump's evangelical advisers, said of the "shithole" comment:

> Apart from the vocabulary attributed to him, President Trump is right on target in his sentiment.
>
> As individual Christians, we have a biblical responsibility to place the needs of others above our own, but as commander in chief, President Trump has the constitutional responsibility to place the interest of our nation above the needs of other countries.
>
> I'm grateful we have a president like Donald Trump who understands that distinction and has the courage to protect the well-being of our nation.
>
> (Scott, 2018)

Power, place, and the spatial dialectic 95

Results from ideological work of journalists explaining and justifying commentary about place that is based on cultural and social divides, misinformation, and sensationalism (although it is hard to explain how such comments from a president is not news) contribute to larger public cognition of geographies and reinforce stereotypes and disinformation that journalists are believed to be addressing.

In addition to the residual racial harm that perpetuates an individual's struggle with negative attitudes and language about their race, home, and other identities (Karmali, Kawakami, and Page-Gould, 2017) there are implications as to how others come to see places via news media. These narratives ultimately inform businesses about where to invest, public officials about which neighborhoods are the best – or worst – for additional resources and gerrymandering, and homeowners and renters who are looking for places to call home.

The spatial dialectic of journalism: Banishment and the right to the story

Historically, newspapers have been housed near downtown districts while TV and radio stations, requiring a larger physical footprint for production space, appear on the edge of town. But each of these entities tend to carry the name of the geographies they are said to cover, placing news media at the center of making place.

The New York Times in New York City, KIYU public radio in Galena, Alaska, which provides "Community Radio for Alaska", and *The Wisconsin State Journal*, which appears at Madison.com in Madison, Wisconsin, are examples of how well media outlets connect – through language, iconography, and call-signs – to their home places. These media names appear in newspaper boxes and on coffee tables throughout a geography, while TV and radio stations boast being a region's No. 1 spot for news, music, and culture.

A village's pulpit, for the churchgoer, served to pronounce explanation for local events, prescribe solutions to the local ills, and to present news from away to those in the vicinity. The ritual of communication, as Carey (2009) tells us, has long been established within the sociability of collectives. The digital element has extended not the role and ritual of communication but has provided the tools and devices used to communicate.

The online world, then, has been a space for emotional and intellectual "awayness" in which the user remains in a physical location – or between physical locations – and operate as a space for representation and exploration of identity (Tuzcu, 2016). This sense of "awayness," we argue, creates an alternative mental and emotional space in which users invest time,

96 *Power, place, and the spatial dialectic*

energy, and other resources while remaining in their physical locations. These elements, and especially the tensions between investments in one's physical and virtual spaces, also move to new forms of power for the self, collectives, and in the role of others to interpret and interfere in perspectives of place.

But in communicative processes of journalistic boundary work related to being the authoritative voice of explanation within specific geographies, journalists, too, operate to keep out particular voices – from within the journalistic interpretive community and outside of it. News practices such as boundary work and shaming (Hess and Gutsche, 2018; Hess and Waller, 2017) function to banish undesirables not only from social and public spheres, but from dominant, journalistic storytelling and explanation of social and cultural life.

As journalistic values and norms of information-gathering, assessment, and production operate in conjunction with fellow social institutions of power maintenance, (i.e., government, police, entertainment and popular culture enterprise, faith communities) those with counter-narratives risk being funneled out of dominant discourse. What remains, then, in journalistic work – in part because of pressures of newswork and in part because of issues of power – are the voices and perspectives of a select few who maintain acceptable social practices and positions.

These voices, therefore, boost fallacies of "community" in a given context in which discourse and contestation appears, but which also exudes elite, dominant articulations of public life and can represent idealistic views of journalistic functions of democratic speech and involvement. Banishment via boosterism (Gutsche, 2015a; 2017) provides some with the "right" to telling stories of geography while keeping others out through shaming and blaming.

The notion of "right to the city" has emerged in critical geography studies since the 1960s in which residents have been identified as holding an inherent right to shape the natural and built environments in the places they live and in ways they incorporate justice for nature, development, and living (Attoh, 2011; Lefebvre, 1991). Critical geographers continue to assess the ability of cities to be open to rights to determine appropriate forms of policing, public and private financing, housing, and environmental justice. Work on this area includes the right of individuals and groups to explore cities by foot (Middleton, 2018) and to create senses of community as groups of newcomers (Garbin and Millington, 2018).

Much of the work that focuses on spatial justice highlights the contestation of a single community as it is defined by power elites. This official place-making – the subject of city-making campaigns by politicians and business leaders, supported by police and educational systems, and distributed and legitimatized by journalists – makes the role of communication an interesting form of violence against difference and diversity within our geographies.

Power, place, and the spatial dialectic 97

The "right to the story," then, is another layer to acknowledging interactions of agency of individuals and of collectives and issues of power, not just about how a city should look or what it should feel like but how it should be imagined. Indeed, imaginations of geographies are normalized frequently in a banal manner. The mottos of "I Think I'm Gonna Like It Here," in Liverpool, UK (Liverpool-one.com, 2018) and "Fields of Opportunity" in Iowa, US (Gutsche, 2012) – serve as otherwise unremarkable statements that indicate an expectation of unity and utopia, which a reasonable person surely cannot adopt outright.

Yet, these mottos further provide meaning to places that provide everyday nods and reminders to what the elite find important, from the arts and "civicness" to the approved social behaviors that individuals must abide by within the geographic boundaries (Green, Grace, and Perkins, 2018).

Bridging geographic divides through narratives of oppression

Journalists are known for reporting on news from across wide geographies and transforming stories of one place in ways that "make sense" for and to audiences from other places. A complication of journalism, in fact, is the role of "being there" (or not) in the creation of knowledge within journalism that serves to inform audiences' perceptions of distant (and local) events through imaginative power and storytelling (Huiberts and Joye, 2017).

Terms such as "firsthand witnessing," "legwork," "eyewitness," and "shoe-leather reporting" have long been associated with journalistic practice and speak to the continued importance of performative proximity that we outlined previously. But these stories, produced "away" from a central newsroom, are riddled with opportunity for interpretations of and for the powerful that either misrepresent or ignore perspectives on what has occurred in and around another place.

Journalists rely on sources for these insights, surely, in order to address multiple viewpoints and to share voices, but they also rely on their own knowledge of what the audience "might think" about stories from given spaces, particularly if those stories do not mesh with dominant understanding of an event, issue, or geography. The 2011 riots throughout London and other parts of England, for instance, provided *The Guardian* newspaper with an opportunity to plot stories of meaning about where, how, and why the events were unfolding, using digital technologies to map both places of violence and people's stories.

This approach attempted to get to the "why" of the violence, which not surprisingly matched those of riots some 40 years earlier – breakdowns in economic and racial relations (see Gutsche, 2017, pp. 214–215). Yet, these answers of "why" and "why there" quickly turned into discussions about "realities" of class and race struggles from levels of the powerful that swept

98 *Power, place, and the spatial dialectic*

the riots and unrest under the rug like ash. Simply, people were suggested to be at fault for their own behaviors, while police, business, and education industries escaped blame. Was this a problem of journalists being unfamiliar with the diversity of geographies and populations, or were the problems just that complicated that simple solutions of blame were assigned? Or, was it a little of both?

Similar patterns of discourse occurred throughout the mid- to late-2010s in the US following resistance to the killing of blacks by white police. In that respect, Gutsche and Estrada (2017) found local news outlets in cities across the US that had experienced their own high-profile killings of black men by white police officers used narrative explanations of urban "disorder" in Baltimore in 2015 to explain away causes for local police killings in their own cities. In other words:

> Narratives and explanations of racialized policing and subsequent protests in Baltimore that appeared in news of local conflict exemplified the fluidity of national, racialized narratives of naturalized police authority to control urban spaces.
>
> (p. 34)

As a result, local journalists explained away moments of racial divide and police violence in their own communities by telling stories about how that couldn't happen "here" – even though it had – by relying on narratives of "big-city" racial violence and social conditions and banishing local counter-narratives by ignoring them. Indeed, the banishment of stories of counter-explanation are common enough, so much so that they are likely by the reader of this book to be seen as unimportant, as journalist's can "tell every story." And, these ideological processes of storytelling that banish and blame are often forgotten by journalists when highly publicized cases of "journalistic awareness" appear.

In April 2018, for example, *National Geographic* attempted reflexivity in its announcement of what the world of magazine readers already knew: lands "faraways" from Western worlds tend to be viewed through mediated imperialistic and colonizing storytelling. Magazine editor Susan Goldberg (2018) wrote this to place the reader in the magazine's long history of racialized reporting:

> It is November 2, 1930, and National Geographic has sent a reporter and a photographer to cover a magnificent occasion: the crowning of Haile Selassie, King of Kings of Ethiopia, Conquering Lion of the Tribe of Judah. There are trumpets, incense, priests, spear-wielding warriors. The story runs 14,000 words, with 83 images.

Power, place, and the spatial dialectic 99

If a ceremony in 1930 honoring a black man had taken place in America, instead of Ethiopia, you can pretty much guarantee there wouldn't have been a story at all. Even worse, if Haile Selassie had lived in the United States, he would almost certainly have been denied entry to our lectures in segregated Washington, D.C., and he might not have been allowed to be a National Geographic member.

Goldberg continued in her introductory article to note that "[i]t hurts to share the appalling stories from the magazine's past," such as a 1916 story from Australia. She writes: "Underneath photos of two Aboriginal people, the caption reads: 'South Australian Blackfellows: These savages rank lowest in intelligence of all human beings.'"

Goldberg – and the April issue – goes on to focus on issues of race within a geographic context and on forms by which the magazine has attempted to change the way its pages focus on race, such as in 2015, in the words of Goldberg, "when we gave cameras to young Haitians and asked them to document the reality of their world." The problem here is the notion of "giving" and the expectation that the producers, then, should express themselves in the ways the magazine most benefits – the selection and production of photographs "from there."

While Goldberg is right, that there has been much improvement in covering the world – and issues – through a more careful lens, the question is the degree to which journalists and audiences are prepared to constantly question appearances in media coverage of the world in terms of "here" and "there" and whether a publication (or its industry) will ever be able to escape the histories in the ways that its purposes and processes of talking about places today change. Nevertheless, the activities of institutions that inform the press – and that in turn are informed by the press – about how to view the world in dominant ways are unlikely to be contested, because of the power system supporting the views.

While naturalized normative acts of telling stories can be examined for their deeper meanings through reflexivity – a process we describe and discuss in the book's conclusion – the process of reflexivity in journalism and what it looks like is likely an area of much debate and about the influence of racism and hegemonic dominant ideologies about how and why journalism functions to "serve" communities, particularly in terms of protecting the vulnerable (Gutsche, 2017).

Conclusion

In this chapter, we have attempted to radicalize the geographies of journalism by introducing notions of the "right to the city" and, more specifically

100   *Power, place, and the spatial dialectic*

to our field and interests, the "right to the story." By discussing elements of inequality in how geographies are defined for "local" and wider audiences through journalism, we have also been able to examine how digital technologies and tools distract audiences – and journalists – from the deeper power of language, story, and narratives of space, place, and explanation.

In the next chapter, we conclude with discussions on the ways in which journalists in particular can address place-making as a power process that identifies the role of technology and, more importantly, the role of culture in creating borders, both physical and ideological, in news.

Notes

1 But, "professional journalists" who take seriously the task of digging deeper into the story – or who have the autonomy to do so – give the white superior doxa oxygen by trying to contextualize the comments for audiences. By doing so, journalists maintain their relevance in terms of providing "the news of the day" and in justifying their selection of that news by paying heed to hate speech, simply because it comes from an official source.

2 Celebrities and popular figures uphold these images of geography – of the Middle East – as a single place of constant conflict without signs of civilization, innovation, and peace, and the United States as a world of "making it," without stories of pain, corruption, and state-issued violence.

3 That journalists remain current in technological innovation, involved in arenas of public discourse surrounding news events, and quick in providing information to audiences, exacts the expectations of news audiences to see journalism, in its traditional sense, as pertinent to social cohesion and as a powerful institution in its own right. One way to measure journalism and the effects of changing practice, therefore, may not be through quantifiable data but on the very value and virtue of journalism.

4 Indeed, the massive move to data and digitization within journalism, including archiving and automation, has contributed to a desire for even more constant and increased watching of audiences as a form of "reporting." However, this watching deepens the role of journalists as masters of social surveillance and does so in ways that diminish critical inquiry about the practices for techo-flash and flair. Journalists the world over are measuring their impact through their roles as social observers, in ways where we can count the public meetings they attend and their record numbers of social media followers, all of which are supported by a commitment to the shaming effect (and clickbate) of the perp walk and entrance of reporters into private homes and spaces for information that the audience "must know."

5 Still, the role of journalism creating spaces and places of surveillance and social control operates in the imagination of the place-name. In the case of "China," for instance, many may have read the above section with a "common sense" understanding that China is a "closed society," one within which actions of travel bans (common enough in "Western" societies) and social metrics (which already exist in the many platforms used daily by journalists and others globally) are not surprisingly products of the "Chinese government." However, such assignment of

Power, place, and the spatial dialectic 101

meaning to a single place-name is a clear outcome of the processes of place-making at the center of this book.
6 Certainly, not all individuals feel shame, but that is not to say that media shaming does not hold members of the public to specific standards of behavior and ideological following. The threat alone of shaming is enough to influence individual behaviors even if the one, herself, is not the subject of shame.

Conclusion
Advancing the research agenda

Our physical geographies, which greatly inform collective understandings of place-names, wayfinding, and geographic definitions, are riddled with socially constructed inequalities, as we have especially identified in the previous chapter. At massive scales, geography is divided into hemispheres and nation states, regions, and named landscapes with political borders established through war, economic conflict, and forced removal and expansion of collectives. Even in the cases where physical walls or fences mark the lines, these borders are human constructs, reified by communication and action.

The stories we tell about how and why borders and boundaries exist and what occurs inside and outside of them are fables of human social action in which natural law is a supporting character. A river becomes an indomitable crossing, a hill or mountain a landmark of meaning. And even with landscapes that are impregnable, stories of ownership and of existence blanket the area. The story of what's "over there" and where the boundary is – even if we haven't been there, haven't ever seen it, and may never go – is unwavering in our minds and social laws.

Within legal and economic systems, property has long been distinguished between public and private and semi-public and semi-private. A shopping mall or arcade may appear to be a public space, designed with passageways, with street corners and sidewalks that in some geographies are designated to be and are owned by "the public." Yet, these spaces are frequently private, surveilled, and secured by private forces, events occurring there controlled, monitored, and placed in memory through corporate influences. Here, speech rights and notions of privacy apply in very different ways, in which the citizen is watched and navigated through systems that reduce their rights and forcefully shape their experiences.

With this book, we hope to start a conversation within journalism studies about geography as it stands in both traditional and new ways of making news. The imagination is a powerful influence on our social policies,

Conclusion 103

personal interactions, and the practice of journalism, so much so that the daily process of place-making in our own lives and in the most banal of news stories becomes embedded, normalized, and made to be less than obvious.

The unpacking of geographies of journalism, then, requires more than just a set of theories, characteristics, and methodologies – it becomes a choice that we make to complicate our most recognized practices to understand how and why we discuss our places and their people. At the same time, this book about geographies encourages a "feet on the ground" approach to studying journalism, to understand the interplay between physical, digital, and virtual worlds and how this all relates to news media.

Building borders: Journalism and the imagination of boundaries

US President Donald Trump's fixation on building a wall to further divide (physically and symbolically) the United States from Mexico (effectively the global North from the South) is perhaps one of the most striking contemporary exemplars of the significance of geography to journalism studies in the digital era. Firstly, the situation in the United States serves as a textbook exemplar for the cultural geographer about how media and politics create cultural binaries around geographic territory, generating ideas related to nationalism and political and cultural divides around identity and place in the interests of power.

Cultural geography is only one part of the picture, however. The patrolled US/Mexican border also cuts through naturally treacherous and difficult landscape, so Trump's wall may have to take new twists and turns to suit the terrain in order to reduce costs, a common thread that appears in news coverage of the wall. Here, the wall's construction is constrained by the natural terrain rather than cultural forces that could reshape the borderline.

Mainstream journalists have become complicit in reinforcing this idea of a difficult, untamed, and dangerous binary between places; the very acceptance and reinforcement via media that the border is a necessary part of the "natural order of things" reinforces political power, and the practice of impartial, objective reporting, too, means that Trump's sensational statements such as "I will build a great wall – and nobody builds walls better than me" are replayed as soundbites across the globe over and over again given their appeal to wider news values of conflict and controversy.

So often, too, journalists report on border politics from a geographic distance, which is also a practice in need of attention. A perception – aided by film and television (think HBO's award-winning series *Breaking Bad*) – enters public discourse that the border is, at the very least, a Wild West that

104 *Conclusion*

needs taming and that those on the "wrong side" have no place in Trump's imagined America. Developments in June 2018 about child detainees in this building of borders has also deepened the emotional element related to border wars in related journalism.

The media's role in covering Trump's plan for a wall also exposes the disruptive tensions between journalism practice and its relationship to place in the digital age. Boundary work can also be particularly useful when examining journalists' interaction with wider social spaces – that is beyond the news media field alone – especially the role of journalists in drawing boundaries around "good" versus "evil" discourse (Gutsche and Salkin, 2017), perception of geographic territory, and shaping understandings of "us" and "them" in geopolitical contexts and local settings. Benedict Anderson's idea of the "imagined community" is today in sharp contrast to Trump's imagined community of America built through divisive language and the demonizing of others.

This presents a conundrum for journalism when it comes to the strategic rituals employed within the profession to maintain legitimacy. The taken-for-granted norm of objectivity and impartial reporting can, by default, reinforce the boundary work performed by political elites around places and territory. The study of boundary work is incomplete, therefore, without a much richer appreciation of journalism's relationship to place.

Addressing perceptions of place in mobile media spheres

While geotechnologies, robot or algorithmic journalism, and reduced-cost mobile technologies and social media venues increased the ability of journalists to do more with less, overcoming barriers of time and distance are still real and intensifying.

Digital journalism that has become exceedingly mobile has extended the role of journalism creation to the citizen in ways that are not generally considered "citizen journalism" but that depend on the perceptions of digitally connected observers of news to contribute to dominant media messages of events, spaces, and places.

Public scenes are captured on video, public data is collected and analyzed, and photographs and audio clips and video are retained by corporate media outlets to be used at their discretion wherever and whenever with sometimes forgotten or lapsed explanations of a news event's geographic connections and complications of media. Additionally, social media has contributed to the continuity of journalism – and perhaps has increased its legitimacy in society – as users spread the news across networks and across wider audiences meanings that can be easily contested or controlled.

Lastly, audiences have since grown from local subscribers or listeners within the reaches of radio waves to listeners, viewers, and users whose

Conclusion 105

clicks are traced and measured from across the globe, contributing to a performance of an omnipresent journalist that has no specific "home," but may, then, have a diluted understanding of many places.

While cultural geography is certainly the more dominant approach for media studies that can be especially helpful in understanding the cultural complexities of mobile media and audiences, there is less attention played to the way people use media in certain contexts to reinforce their own perceptions about places and how people use media to go about their daily lives and facilitate social order.

While social geography has been influenced by the cultural turn there is a point of distinction between the two exemplified by the role local media play at the Mexican/US border, for instance. Michael Dear argues that those living at the border are, in fact, more connected than divided. He gives the example of San Diego-Tijuana – the busiest port on the borderline, processing an average of 70,000 Northbound vehicle passengers and 20,000 Northbound pedestrians per day:

> Border crossers have become accustomed to delays imposed by the wall, and tune into media to factor them into their commutes. You might see agricultural workers driving at 4 a.m. from Mexicali, Mexico to fields in the Imperial Valley. Or, parents of Mexican children organizing early morning carpools to ferry their kids to school in Calexico, California using special passes that speed up the commute. They've learned how to cope.
>
> (Dear, 2017)

Here, the role of media to facilitate social order among and about a global society that has become familiar with enhanced mobility is integral to the daily lives of everyday people, uniquely located at the intersection of politically and culturally separated worlds. The point here is that there exist immense advantages to those media platforms we turn to not just to help us construct understandings or perceptions of places but for those that provide the reliable, place-based knowledge and information that shapes our daily actions, even when issues of inequality are subtly reinforced in this process.

Indeed, geographic wayfinding – navigating where to go, how to get there, and what one experiences along the way – also becomes especially influenced based upon the everyday understandings and interpretations of space and place via media. Beyond the narratives of place that journalists provide audiences, which inform how and where audience members travel, a user-informed GPS program that navigates around the shamed "bad neighborhoods" – or alternative trails that move publics around neighborhoods or to destinations informed by businesses or paid avenues – is a product (and perhaps an expectation) of today's digital user (Keyes, 2012).

106   *Conclusion*

Digital journalism operates in a similar manner of informing wayfinding online by directing users to information based upon which searches, "likes," shares, and comments are popular. In the end, the use of SEO by journalists not only influences which of their content is seen but influences what is publicly depicted as unpopular or shouldn't be missed based on what is "popular" and "appropriate." SEO also purposefully banishes certain minority voices (Noble, 2018). This staging and stacking of information – via narratives of "good places" and "bad," of what is legitimate or popular and what is not – reflects a notion of spatial dialectic and banishment.

A media geography approach to understanding the influence of mobility, technology, and digital audiences should inspire studies that encourage journalists to offer a critical reflection of how movement at and across borders is portrayed in news media. Adams (2018), for example, has highlighted that maps that show migration movements should be studied through technologies of critical cartography which seek to analyze, interpret, and contextualize cartography as a social practice. Importantly to the geographies of journalism, Adams also highlights research that identifies the way mapping can offer the progressive capacity to imagine places anew (see also Nikunen, 2016).

Processes of mental mapping in journalism (Gutsche, 2015a; 2017) that identify the wayfinding and place-making of citizens, journalists, and official sources, for instance, can easily be replicated by scholars and adopted by journalists to understand the "communities" that they cover.

Additionally, the notion of "affective geographies" (Giaccardi and Fogli, 2008) also provides opportunities for web mapping to go beyond showing geographic locations and connections between people via those maps to the meanings embedded within the locations depicted and the relationships formed.

At its heart though, this book is about how news media serve as place-makers and generate perceptions of places. That means not only the creation of place representations but how everyday people become involved in the place-making process themselves. Audience-centred approaches to news, such as those spearheaded by scholars like Irene Costera Meijer, are useful because they emphasize that approaching web metrics, professional values, and user-generated content from the angle of the audience, users, and participants helps to avoid a systematic bias and understand what journalism is through the eyes of others (see especially Costera Meijer and Groot Kormelink, 2016)

Of any epistemological position that compliments such approaches to understanding both relationships – that is, the geographic locations of culture and socio-politics, and the contestations – it is within cultural anthropology. We call for a return to "media anthropology" within journalism

Conclusion 107

studies, therefore, to place within the field a center on cultural studies and qualitative methodologies that can bring to light issues of power, oppression, and resistance (Pertierra, 2018; Rothenbuhler and Coman, 2005).

Media researchers and journalists alike must also find a way to make "scholarship" meaningful and applicable to address issues of power in place-making through journalistic reflexivity.

Journalistic reflexivity in place-making

Let us root our call above in a solid example here. From the opening of a new business to a murder scene, our neighborhoods and street corners become transfixed by TV cameras and reporters with note pads and cell phones. On the ground, journalists trickle in as the news event develops, and in a poof when it's over these spaces are returned to what they were – a street corner now with a bit more litter. Yet, in the new media news age, two specific marks are left when reporters leave – or when the neighborhood is finally left out of the news cycle – and the dissection of these actions and results are critical to the reflexive journalist who attempts to understand how her story shapes geographic imaginations.

First, it becomes critical for journalists to understand the influence of digital geography on expanding to a wider audience that becomes exposed to a portion (or an interpretation) of a particular geography of which they may never have a personal experience. Reporting on a neighborhood shooting, a robbery, or even an opening of a business, for instance, reveals only narratives associated with the events of that time in that space to these audiences, making the interpretation of the space by the journalist even more critical to understand.

Rarely do journalists, themselves, expand beyond or vary greatly from shared routines of their industry and coverage areas and narratives so much so that news outlets tell different stories from the same news event from the same space, meaning that audiences can get the "same story" of a geography from multiple sources. And as a result, limitations of geographic meanings exposed during media narratives of these locations in terms of the selection and exclusion of information, vantage points, images, and explanations become especially important in that they may be the only ones that members of the audience will have at the time or in future times, which deepens the lasting impact of meaning for those audience members.

When these narratives are sent across social networks and into widening audiences – as nearly any check of a Google News search or a trending feed of Facebook or Twitter shows – the media become an echo chamber of voices, perspectives, and meanings of a select few for a very many. Audiences, then, are left with single interpretations of the world – and of a

108 *Conclusion*

single part of the world – that are perhaps altered in slight physical senses of images and sounds but narrow in how they may have been described and explained to audiences.

Second, journalists should be aware that spaces they cover are left exposed to public memory of geography, and collectives' right to be forgotten is left vulnerable to reproduction, sharing, and used in algorithms of what's considered news – its names, geographies, and images placed in public news morgues for adoption in the creation of public policy, policing, and economy. Reporters harbor go-to points where they "know" news to happen based on history or where they can find information, including in simple practices of clip searches that inform journalists what has happened in a particular location over time, at least as "seen" by journalists.

Relatedly, how previous stories explain social conditions proves especially problematic for journalists in discussing news and news spaces of the past. A journalist would have a difficult time explaining social conditions and issues of a geography widely differently than a journalist of yesterday, as each representation of explanation grounds knowledge of today in meanings of the past.

A new idea, such as "solutions journalism" – that which positions both causes and potential problem-solving at the center of the coverage, rather than merely the conflict itself – has complicated the role of journalism and geography in an attempt to be reflexive about how journalism interacts with solutions and problems. However, in covering "another's" culture in making these connections visible, it becomes problematic to provide solutions based on one's own values, experiences, and solutions.

Journalists in a city center and who have little personal or journalistic experience covering rural issues and daily life will rarely have adequate positionality to solve problems. White journalists, too, may be sympathetic and appreciative of challenges of those of another skin tone – even in the same geography. However, the lived experience of white journalists and the "Other" (as non-whites are frequently depicted in news) only fuels the journalists' imagination of racial struggle, living, resistance, and banality.

Even in a digital age when online fora, social media (including Black Twitter), and expanded opportunities for expression via virtual reality may help journalists bridge divides in understanding (Longhi, 2017), the colonial spirit of news provides a gaze by which the institution of journalism and its audience address problems and maintain a geographic dimension (Jones, 2017).

Increased views of the world, of conflict, of advancements through drone and CCTV footage, soundbites, and video clips of events that happen far beyond our doorsteps enhance our thoughts of what "could" be happening

Conclusion 109

somewhere else, and why, informed by our imaginations and subjectivities, the danger a process of verisimilitude and attachments to violence.

In this process, the effected lives are pixels or pixelated, the outcomes of policies and public actions diluted via a hope for "the right thing" to have happened. The changes to journalism – and to journalism studies – have entered into a discussion of time in that cultural shifts take care and experimentation, but are also mired in attention to "innovation" and new-ness (Carlson and Lewis, 2018).

Still, we have strong hopes for the desire and abilities of scholars and practicing journalists alike to identify and make change, though to do so, the world of journalism might look very different. It starts by repositioning journalists as much more than conduits of information. They are the place-makers of the digital age.

References

Adams, P. (2018). Migration maps with the news: Guidelines for ethical visualisation of mobile populations. *Journalism Studies*, 19(4), 527–547.

Adams, P., Craine, J., & Dittmer, D. (2014). *The Ashgate Research Companion to Media Geography*. Sussex, UK: Ashgate.

Ahva, L. & Pantti, M. (2014). Proximity as a journalistic keyword in the digital era: A study on the "closeness" of amateur news images. *Digital Journalism*, 2(3), 322–333.

Alexander, B. (2016, 15 November). Dev Patel joyously reunites with his "lion co-star after visa battle". *USA Today*. Accessed 23 April 2018 at www.usatoday.com/story/life/movies/2016/11/15/indian-star-lion-visa-battle-sunny-pawar/93906830.

Ali, C. (2016). Critical regionalism and the polities of place: Revisiting localism for the digital age. *Communication Theory*, 26, 106–127.

Anderson, B. (1983). *Imagined Communities: Reflections on the Origin and Spread of Nationalism*. London: Verso.

Anderson, C. & Maeyer, J. (2014). Objects of journalism and the news. *Journalism*, 16(1), 3–9.

Appadurai, A. (2001). Grassroots globalisation and the research imagination. In A. Appadurai (Ed.), *Globalisation* (pp. 1–21). Durham, NC: Duke University Press.

Appelgren, E. (2017). An illusion of interactivity: The paternalistic side of data journalism. *Journalism Practice*. Doi: 10.1080/17512786.2017.1299032.

Arnould, E. J. & Thompson, C. J. (2015). Introduction: Consumer culture theory: Ten years gone (and beyond). In A. E. Thyroff, J. B. Murray, & R. W. Belk (Eds.), *Consumer Culture Theory* (pp. 1–21). Bingley, UK: Emerald.

Associated Press. (2018, 14 March). What was Joe Biden talking about with homeless man? Accessed 10 April 2018 at www.mercurynews.com/2018/03/14/photoshows-joe-biden-with-homeless-man-outside-theater.

Attoh, K. A. (2011). What kind of right is the right to the city? *Progress in Human Geography*, 35, 669–685.

Australian Broadcasting Corporation. (2018, 20 March). ABC South West Victoria Facebook page. Accessed at www.facebook.com/abcsouthwestvic/.

Australian Communications Media Authority. Accessed at www.acma.gov.au.

Balakrishnan, A., Salinas, S., & Hunter, M. (2018, 21 March). Mark Zuckerberg has been talking about privacy for 15 years. *CNBC*. Accessed 23 April 2018 at

References   111

www.cnbc.com/2018/03/21/facebook-ceo-mark-zuckerbergs-statements-on-privacy-2003-2018.html.

Barthes, R. (1972). *Mythologies*. New York: Hill and Wang.

Baudrillard, J. (1983). *Simulations*. New York: Scmiotext(e).

Bauman, Z. (1998). *Globalisation the Human Consequences*. Cambridge: Polity Press.

Bhabha, H. K. (1990). *Nation and Narration*. New York: Routledge.

Boden, D. & Molotch, H. (1994). The compulsion to proximity. In R. Friedland & D. Boden (Eds.), *Nowhere: Space, Time and Modernity* (pp. 257–286). Berkeley: University of California Press.

Bødker, H. & Neverla, I. (2012). Introduction: Environmental journalism. *Journalism Studies*, 13(2), 152–156.

Bødker, H. & Ngomba, T. (2018). Community repair through truce and contestation. *Journalism Studies*, 19(4), 579–593.

Boltanski, L. (1999). *Distant Suffering: Morality, Media and Politics*. Cambridge: Cambridge University Press.

Bork-Huffer, T. (2017). Mediated sense of place: Effects of mediation and mobility on the place perception of German professionals in Singapore. *New Media and Society*, 18(1), 2155–2170.

Bourdieu, P. (1977). *Outline of a Theory of Practice*. Cambridge: Cambridge University Press.

Bourdieu, P. (1984). *Distinction: A Social Critique of the Judgement of Taste*. Cambridge: Harvard University Press.

Bourdieu, P. (1989). Social space and symbolic power. *Sociological Theory*, 7, 14–25.

Bourdieu, P. (1999). *The Weight of the World: Social Suffering in Contemporary Society*. Oxford: Polity Press.

Bourdieu, P. (2001). *Masculine Domination*. Cambridge: Polity Press.

Bourdieu, P. (2005). *The Social Structures of the Economy*. Cambridge: Polity Press.

Bourdieu, P. & Passeron, J. C. (2000). *Reproduction in Education, Society and Culture*. London: Sage.

Bourdieu, P. & Thompson, J. B. (1991). *Language and Symbolic Power*. Cambridge & Malden, MA: Polity Press.

Bruns, A. (2014). Media innovations, user innovations, societal innovations. *The Journal of Media Innovations*, 1(1), 13–27.

Bulkeley, W. (1998, 16 November). Corporate sneers: Who knows better what the future holds than those who make a living about it? *The Wall Street Journal*.

Buni, C. (2016, 16 November). What exactly is Facebook? *The Verge*. Accessed 23 April 2018 at www.theverge.com/2016/11/16/13655102/facebook-journalism-ethics-media-company-algorithm-tax.

Burgess, J. A. & Gold, J. R. (1985). *Geography, the Media and Popular Culture*. London: Croom Helm.

Cai, G. & Tian, Y. (2016, 31 October). Towards geo-referencing infrastructure for local news. Paper presented at the 10th workshop on geographic information retrieval, Association for Computing Machinery, California.

Carey, J. W. (1977). Mass communication and cultural studies. In *Communication as Culture: Essays on Media and Society* (pp. 37–68). London: Routledge.

112 References

Carey, J. W. (2009). *Communication as Culture*. New York: Routledge.

Carlson, M. & Lewis, S. C. (2015). *Boundaries of Journalism: Professionalism, Practices and Participation*. London: Routledge.

Carlson, M. & Lewis, S. C. (2018). Temporal reflexivity in journalism studies: Making sense of change in a more timely fashion. *Journalism*. Doi: 10.1177/1464884918760675.

Carlton, S. (2018, 7 March). To give or not to give: Should you hand over a dollar to a homeless person on a street corner? *Tampa Bay Times*. Accessed 23 April 2018 at www.tampabay.com/news/To-give-or-not-to-give-Should-you-hand-over-a-dollar-to-a-homeless-person-on-a-street-corner-_165186739.

Casino, V. (2009). *Social Geography: A Critical Introduction*. West Sussex, UK: Wiley Blackwell.

Castells, M. (2010). *The Rise of the Network Society: With a New Preface*. Oxford: Wiley-Blackwell.

Christensen, M. & Jansson, A. (2014). Complicit surveillance, interveillance, and the question of cosmopolitanism: Toward a phenomenological understanding of mediatization. *New Media & Society*, 17(9), 1473–1491.

Clancy, C. (2014). The politics of temporality: Autonomy, temporal spaces and resoluteness. *Time and Society*, 23(1), 28–48.

Cole, D. (2018, 10 March). Biden seen chatting it up with a homeless man in Washington. *CNN*. Accessed 23 April 2018 at https://edition.cnn.com/2018/03/10/politics/joe-biden-homeless-man-georgetown-photo/index.html.

Cosgrove, D. & Daniels, S. (1988). *The Iconography of Landscape: Essays on the Symbolic Representation, Design and Use of Past Environments*. Cambridge: Cambridge University Press.

Cosgrove, D. & Jackson, P. (1987). New directions in cultural geograp. *Area*, 19, 95–101.

Costera Meijer, I. & Groot Kormelink, T. (2016). Revisiting the audience turn in journalism: How a user-based approach changes the meaning of clicks, transparency and citizen participation. In B. Franklin & S. Eldridge, II (Eds.), *The Routledge Companion to Digital Journalism Studies* (pp. 345–353). Abingdon: Routledge.

Cottle, S. (2006). Mediatised rituals: Beyond manufacturing consent. *Media Culture and Society*, 28(3), 411–432.

Couldry, N. (2000). *The Place of Media Power: Pilgrims and Witnesses of the Media Age*. London: Routledge.

Couldry, N. (2003). *Media Rituals: A Critical Approach*. London: Routledge.

Couldry, N. & Curran, J. (2003). The paradox of media power. In N. Couldry & J. Curran (Eds.), *Contesting Media Power: Alternative Media in a Networked World* (pp. 3–17). Oxford: Rowman & Littlefield Publishers.

Couldry, N. & Hepp, A. (2017). *The Mediated Construction of Reality*. Cambridge: Polity Press.

Craine, J. (2016). Media geography. *Oxford Bibliographies*. Accessed 23 April 2018 at www.oxfordbibliographies.com/view/document/obo-9780199874002/obo-9780199874002-0101.xml.

Cresswell, T. (1996). *In Place Out of Place: Geography, Ideology and Transgression*. Minneapolis, MN: University of Minnesota Press.

References 113

Cresswell, T. (2010). New cultural geography: An unfinished project. *Cultural Geographies*, 17(2), 169–174.

Daniels, G. L. & Loggins, D. M. (2010). Data, doppler, or depth of knowledge: How do television stations differentiate local weather? *Atlantic Journal of Communication*, 18(1), 22–35.

Dash, K. N. (2004). *Invitation to Social and Cultural Anthropology*. Rajouri Garden, New Dehli: Atlantic.

Davidson, D. (2018, 21 March). Truth to triumph in Google's new news algorithm. *The Australian*. P. 21.

Davies, N. (2009). *Flat Earth News: An Award-Winning Reporter Exposes Falsehood, Distortion and Propaganda in the Global Media*. London: Vintage.

Davis O'Brien, R. (2010, 9 August). Zuckerberg at Harvard: The truth behind the social network. *The Daily Beast*. Accessed 23 April 2018 at www.thedailybeast.com/mark-zuckerberg-at-harvard-the-truth-behind-the-social-network.

Dear, M. (2017, 6 March). Americans and Mexicans living at the border are more connected than divided. *The Conversation*. Accessed 23 April 2018 at https://theconversation.com/americans-and-mexicans-living-at-the-border-are-more-connected-than-divided-72348.

Deleuze, G. & Guattari, F. (1988). *A Thousand Plateaus: Capitalism and Schizophrenia*. London: Athlone.

DeLoach, T. (2018). The effects of mediatized hate: Coping with life in Trumpland. In R. E. Gutsche, Jr. (Ed.), *The Trump Presidency, Journalism, and Democracy* (pp. 299–310). New York & Oxon, UK: Routledge.

Derickson, K. D. (2017). Urban geography II: Urban geography in the age of Ferguson. *Progress in Human Geography*, 41(2), 230–234.

Deuze, M. & Witschge, T. (2017). Beyond journalism: Theorising the transformation of journalism. *Journalism*. Doi: 10.1177/1464884916688550.

Doss, E. (2002). Death, art and memory in the public sphere: The visual and material culture of grief in contemporary America. *Mortality*, 7, 63–82.

Dowd, M. (2017, 16 December). Bringing down our monsters. *The New York Times*. Accessed 23 April 2018 at www.nytimes.com/2017/12/16/opinion/sunday/sexual-harassment-salma-hayek.html.

Duarte, F. (2017). *Space Place and Territory: A Critical Review on Spatialities*. New York: Routledge.

Dutton, W. & Dubois, E. (2015). The Fifth Estate: A rising force of pluralistic accountability. In S. Coleman & D. Freelon (Eds.), *Handbook of Digital Politics* (pp. 51–66). Northampton: Edward Elgar Publishing.

English, T. J. (2011). *The Savage City: Race, Murder, and a Generation on the Edge*. New York: HarperCollins.

Ettema, J. S. (2005). Crafting cultural resonance: Imaginative power in everyday journalism. *Journalism*, 6(2), 131–152.

Feik, N. (2017, 1 July). Killing our news media. *The Monthly*. Accessed 23 April 2018 at www.themonthly.com.au/issue/2017/july/1498831200/nick-feik/killing-our-media.

Freeman, J. & Park, S. (2017). Broadband connectivity for rural communities and farm development. *Farm Policy Journal*, 14(3), 19–29.

114 References

Fry, K. (2003). *Constructing the Heartland: Television News and Natural Disaster.* Cresskill, NJ: Hampton Press.

Fullerton, J. (2018, 24 March). China's "social credit" system bans millions from travelling. *The Telegraph.* Accessed 12 April 2018 at www.telegraph.co.uk/news/2018/03/24/chinas-social-credit-system-bans-millions-travelling.

Gans, H. (2004). *Deciding What's News: A Study of CBS Evening News, NBC Nightly News, Newsweek and Time.* Evanston, IL: Northwestern University Press.

Garbin, D. & Millington, G. (2018). "Central London under siege": Diaspora, "race" and the right to the (global) city. *The Sociological Review,* 66(1), 138–154.

Ghosh, S. (2018, 9 April). Apple cofounder Steve Wozniak is quitting Facebook over data and privacy concerns. *Business Insider.* Accessed 11 April 2018 at http://uk.businessinsider.com/apple-cofounder-steve-wozniak-quit-facebook-2018-4?r=US&IR=T.

Giaccardi, E. & Fogli, D. (2008, 28 May). Affective geographies: Toward richer cartographic semantics for the geospatial web. Paper presented at the International Conference on Advanced Visual Interfaces, Napoli, Italy. Accessed at http://l3d.cs.colorado.edu/~giaccard/research/pdf/GiaccardiFogli_AVI08.pdf.

Goffman, E. (1959). *The Presentation of Self.* New York: Random House.

Goggin, G., Martin, F., & Dwyer, T. (2015). Locative news: Mobile media, place informatics and digital news. *Journalism Studies,* 16(1), 41–59.

Goldberg, S. (2018, April). For decades, our coverage was racist: To rise above our past, we must acknowledge it. *National Geographic.* Accessed 23 April 2018 at www.nationalgeographic.com/magazine/2018/04/from-the-editor-race-racism-history.

Goodin, R., Rice, J., Parpo, A., & Eriksson, L. (2008). *Discretionary Time: A New Measure of Freedom.* Cambridge: Cambridge University Press.

Goss, B. M. (2015). The world is not enough: An analysis of Us/Them dichotomies in the *International Herald Tribune/International New York Times. Journalism Studies,* 16(2), 243–258.

Graham, G. (2015, 9 December). Tulsa neighborhoods stuck in identity crisis. *Tulsa World.* Accessed 23 April 2018 at www.tulsaworld.com/news/ginniegraham/gin nie-graham-tulsa-neighborhoods-stuck-in-identity-%20crisis/article_1639e32b-1029-5102-b53f-55d1e0282420.html.

Green, A. (2018, 5 February). Digital distractions are making us dumb and twitchy. *Financial Times.* Accessed 12 April 2018 at www.ft.com/content/e70a58f0-db69-11e7-9504-59efdb70e12f.

Green, A., Grace, D., & Perkins, H. (2018). City elements propelling city brand meaning-making processes: Urban reminders, the arts, and residential behavior. *Marketing Theory.* Doi: 10.1177/14705931177553978.

Gutsche, Jr., R. (2012). "This ain't the ghetto": Diaspora, discourse, and dealing with "Iowa Nice". *Poroi,* 8(2).

Gutsche, Jr., R. E. (2014a). *A Transplanted Chicago: Race, Place and the Press in Iowa City.* Jefferson, NC: McFarland.

Gutsche, Jr., R. E. (2014b). There's no place like home: Storytelling of war in Afghanistan and street crime "at home" in the *Omaha World-Herald. Journalism Practice,* 8(1), 65–79.

References 115

Gutsche, Jr., R. E. (2015a). Boosterism as banishment: Identifying the power function of local, business news and coverage of city spaces. *Journalism Studies*, 16(4), 497–512.

Gutsche, Jr., R. E. (2015b). Sea level rise app launched: What's SLR mean to you? Accessed 16 April 2018 at http://digitalcommons.fiu.edu/cgi/viewcontent.cgi?article=1029&context=sea_level_rise.

Gutsche, Jr., R. E. (2017). *Media Control: News as an Institution of Power and Social Control*. New York & London: Bloomsbury.

Gutsche, Jr., R. E. (2018). News boundaries of "fakiness" and the challenged imaginative power of journalistic authority. In R. E. Gutsche, Jr. (Ed.), *The Trump Presidency, Journalism and Democracy* (pp. 39–58). New York & Oxon, UK: Routledge.

Gutsche, Jr., R. E. & Estrada, C. (2017). Renewing the lease: How news characterizations of Baltimore realigned white reign of US cities. In Linda Steiner and Silvio Waisbord (Eds.), *News of Baltimore: Race, Rage and the City*. New York & Abington: Routledge, pp. 21–40.

Gutsche, Jr., R. E. & Salkin, E. (2017). Behold the monster: Mythical explanations of deviance and evil in news of the Amish school shooting. *Journalism*, 18(8), 994–1010.

Gutsche, Jr., R. E. & Salkin, E. R. (2013). "It's better than blaming a dead young man": Creating mythical archetypes in local coverage of the Mississippi River drownings. *Journalism*, 14(1), 61–77.

Gutsche, Jr., R. E. & Salkin, E. R. (2016). Who lost what? An analysis of myth, loss, and proximity in news coverage of the Steubenville rape. *Journalism*, 17(4), 456–473.

Habermas, J. (1984). *The Theory of Communicative Action*. Boston: Beacon Press.

Hall, E. T. (1959). *The Silent Language*. Greenwich: Fawcett Premier.

Hall, S. (1980). Encoding/decoding. In S. Hall, D. Hobson, A. Lowe, & P. Willis (Eds.), *Culture, Media, Language* (pp. 128–138). London: Hutchinson.

Hare, K. (2018, 11 April). *The Seattle Times* is making it everyone's job to grow subscribers. *Poynter*. Accessed 12 April 2018 at www.poynter.org/news/seattle-times-making-it-everyones-job-to-grow-digital-subscribers.

Harvey, D. (1989). *The Condition of Postmodernity: An Inquiry into the Origins of Social Change*. Cambridge: Blackwell.

Heaton, J. (2004). *Reworking Qualitative Data*. London: Sage.

Hedges, C. (2018, 19 March). Google, Facebook, algorithms, and the building of the iron wall. *Common Dreams*. Accessed 11 April at www.commondreams.org/views/2018/03/19/google-facebook-algorithms-and-building-iron-wall.

Heidegger, M. (1927). *Being and Time*, Translated by J. Macquairre & E. Robinson (1978). New York: Harper and Row.

Henson, R. (2010). *Weather on the Air: A History of Broadcast Meteorology*. Boston: American Meteorological Society.

Hern, A. & Rawlinson, K. (2018, 14 March). Facebook bans Britain First and its leaders. *The Guardian*. Accessed 23 April 2018 at www.theguardian.com/world/2018/mar/14/facebook-bans-britain-first-and-its-leaders.

Herwig, J. (2009, 9 October). Liminality and communitas in social media: The case of twitter. Paper presented at the Internet research 10.0: Critical annual conference

116 References

of the Association of Internet researchers, Milwaukee. Accessed 25 April 2018 at https://digiom.files.wordpress.com/2009/10/herwig_ir10_liminalitycommunitas twitter_v5oct09.pdf.

Hesmondhalgh, D. & Baker, S. (2001). *Creative Labour: Media Work in Three Cultural Industries.* London: Routledge.

Hess, K. (2013). Breaking boundaries: Recasting the small newspaper as geo-social news. *Digital Journalism*, 1(1), 45–60.

Hess, K. (2015). Ritual power: Illuminating the births, deaths and marriages column in news media research. *Journalism*, 17(4), 511–526.

Hess, K. (2016). Power to the virtuous. Civic culture in the changing digital terrain. *Journalism Studies*, 17(7), 925–934.

Hess, K. (forthcoming). Mining the depleted rivers of gold: Public notices and the sustainability of Australian local news in a digitized democracy. In A. Schapals, A. Bruns, & B. McNair (Eds.), *Digitizing Democracy.* London: Routledge.

Hess, K. (2017a). Shifting foundations: Journalism and the power of the common good. *Journalism*, 18(7), 801–816.

Hess, K. (2017b). Mixed fortunes: An examination of circulation rise and decline in two Victorian newspapers. Victorian Country Press Association, Research Report, Melbourne, 1–25.

Hess, K. & Gutsche, Jr., R. E. (2018). Journalism and the social sphere: Rethinking a foundational concept beyond politics and public life. *Journalism Studies*, 19(4), 483–498.

Hess, K. & Waller, L. (2014). Geo-social journalism: Reorienting the study of small commercial newspapers in a digital environment. *Journalism Practice*, 8(2), 121–136.

Hess, K. & Waller, L. (2017). *Local Journalism in a Digital World.* London: Palgrave MacMillan.

Hodgekiss, A. (2015, 18 March). The rise of iPad neck. *Daily Mail Australia.* Accessed 23 April 2018 at www.dailymail.co.uk/health/article-2997339/The-rise-iPad-neck-Tablets-three-times-strain-muscles-desktop-computers.html.

Houlihan, R. (2018, 25 March). Call for inquiry into power companies. *The Standard.* Accessed 23 April 2018 at www.standard.net.au/story/5304680/prime-minister-visits-cobden-call-for-inquiry-after-bushfires-photos-video.

Huiberts, E. & Joye, S. (2017). Close, but not close enough?: Audience's reactions to domesticated distant suffering in international news coverage. *Media, Culture & Society.* Doi: 10.1177/0163443717707342.

Huxford, J. (2007). The proximity paradox: Live reporting, virtual prpoximity and the ocncept of place in the news. *Journalism*, 8(6), 657–674.

Jaffe, J. (2017, 20 October). Defining "Downstate" Illinois. *ProPublica Illinois.* Accessed 16 April 2018 at www.propublica.org/article/defining-downstate-illinois.

Johnson, C. & Hawbaker, K. (2018, 28 March). #METOO: A timeline of events. *Chicago Tribune.* Accessed at www.chicagotribune.com/lifestyles/ct-me-too-timeline-20171208-htmlstory.html.

Johnson, S. & Galloway, S. (2018, 28 February). Young Harvey Weinsten: The making of a monster. *The Hollywood Reporter.* Accessed at www.hollywoodreporter.com/features/young-harvey-weinstein-making-a-monster-1089069.

References 117

Jones, A. (2017). Disrupting the narrative: Immersive journalism in virtual reality. *Journal of Media Practice*, 18(2–3), 171–185.

Karmali, F., Kawakami, K., & Page-Gould, E. (2017). He said what?: Physiological and cognitive responses to imagining and witnessing outgroup racism. *Journal of Experimental Psychology*, 146(8), 1073–1085.

Kearney, R. (2003). *The Wake of Imagination*. New York: Routledge.

Keyes, A. (2012, 19 January). This app was made for walking: But is it racist? *National Public Radio*. Accessed 16 April 2018 at www.npr.org/2012/01/25/145337346/this-app-was-made-for-walking-but-is-it-racist.

Klein, P. W. & Plaut, S. (2017). "Fixing" the journalist-fixer relationship. *Neiman Reports*. Accessed 23 April 2018 at http://niemanreports.org/articles/fixing-the-journalist-fixer-relationship/.

Kleinman, Z. (2018, 21 March). Cambridge Analytica: The story so far. *BBC*. Accessed at www.bbc.com/news/technology-43465968.

Kogen, L. (2017). News you can use or news that moves?: Journalists' rationales for coverage of distant suffering. *Journalism Practice*. Doi: 10.1080/17512786.2017.1400395.

Kreglow, K. (2015, 15 May). Every time you check your phone it's like putting a German Shepherd on your head. *Men's Health*. Accessed 23 April 2018 at www.menshealth.com/health/a19540582/dangers-of-staring-at-smart-phone-all-day.

Langellier, K. M. (2010). Performing Somali identity in the diaspora: "Wherever I go I know who I am". *Cultural Studies*, 24(1), 66–94.

Lash, S. & Urry, J. (1994). *Economies of signs and space*. Sage, Thousand Oaks, California.

Latham, A. (2008). Research, performance, and doing human geography: Some reflections on the diary-photo diary-interview method. In T. Oakes & P. Price (Eds.), *The Cultural Geography Reader* (pp. 68–75). New York: Routledge.

Latour, B. (2005). *Reassembling the Social*. Oxford: Oxford University Press.

Lefebvre, H. (1991). *The Production of Space*. Malden, MA: Blackwell.

Lehtola, V. V. & Ståhle, P. (2014). Societal innovation at the interface of state and civil society. *Innovation*, 27(2), 152–174.

Lemos, A. (2010). Post mass media functions, locative media and informational territories, new ways of thinking about territory, place and mobility in contemporary society. *Space and Culture*, 13(4), 403–420.

Li, M. (2017). Staging a social drama: Ritualised framing of the spring festival homecoming in Chinese state media. *Journalism*. Doi: 10.1177/1464884917704090.

Liverpool-one.com. (2018). I think I'm gonna like it here. *Liverpool One*. Accessed 11 April 2018 at www.liverpool-one.com/inspire-me/i-think-im-gonna-like.

Longhi, R. R. (2017). Immersive narratives in web journalism: Between interfaces and virtual reality. *Estudos em Cominicacão*, 25(1), 13–22.

Lule, J. (2001). *Daily News, Eternal Stories: The Mythological Role of Journalism*. New York: Guilford Press.

Massey, D. (1991). A global sense of place. *Marxism Today*, 38, 24–29.

Massey, D. (1994). *Space, Place and Gender*. Cambridge, US: Polity Press.

118 References

McCoy-McDeid, R. (2018, 6 February). Iowa nice hasn't stopped profiling. *The Cedar Rapids Gazette.* Accesed 23 April 2018 at www.thegazette.com/subject/opinion/guest-columnist/iowa-nice-hasnt-stopped-profiling-20180206.

McGaughy, L. (2017, 9 November). Dear Sutherland Springs, you deserve an apology from the news media. *Dallas Morning News.* Accessed 23 April 2018 at www.dallasnews.com/opinion/commentary/2017/11/09/dear-sutherland-springs-deserve-apology-news-media.

McGoogan, C. (2017, 11 October). Mark Zuckerberg apologies for "tasteless" Puerto Rico VR video. *The Telegraph.* Accessed 23 April 2018 at www.telegraph.co.uk/technology/2017/10/10/mark-zuckerberg-criticised-tasteless-puerto-rico-vr-video.

McLemore, D. (2016, 1 September). Why did media ignore flooding in Louisiana? *Dylanmclemore.com.* Accessed 23 April 2018 at https://dylanmclemore.com/2016/09/01/why-did-media-ignore-flooding-in-louisiana.

McLuhan, M., Fiore, Q., & Agel, J. (2001). *The medium is the massage: An inventory of effects.* Ginko Press, Corte Madera, CA.

McNair, B. (2018). *Fake News: Falsehood, Fabrication and Fantasy in Journalism.* London: Routledge.

Mencher, M. (2010). *News: Reporting and Writing.* New York: McGraw Hill.

Meyrowitz, J. (1985). *No Sense of Place: The Impact of Electronic Media on Social Behaviour.* London: Oxford University Press.

Middleton, J. (2018). The socialities of everyday urban walking and the "right to the city". *Urban Studies,* 55(2), 296–315.

Mills, C. W. (2000). *The Sociological Imagination.* Oxford: Oxford University Press.

Monmonier, M. (1997). *Cartographies of Danger: Mapping Hazards in America.* Chicago & London: University of Chicago Press.

Moores, S. (2012). *Media, Place and Mobility.* New York: Palgrave MacMillan.

Morley, D. (2000). *Home Territories: Media Mobility and Identity.* London & New York: Routledge.

Morley. D. (2006). *Media Modernity and Technology: The Geography of the New.* London: Routledge.

Neal, M., Miles, D., & Martin, S. (2018, 20 March). Victoria and New South Wales bushfires: Poor mobile coverage puts lives at risk. *ABC News.* Accessed 23 April 2018 at www.abc.net.au/news/2018-03-20/mobile-phone-blackspots-put-lives-at-risk-during-fires/9566338.

Newton, G. (2013, 30 January). Go local, would-be journalist! There's a great world outside the national media. *The Guardian.* Accessed 23 April 2018 at www.theguardian.com/uk/the-northerner/2013/jan/30/young-journalists-training-internships-newspapers-media.

The New York Times. (2018, 11 April). nytvr. Accessed 11 April 2018 at www.nytimes.com/marketing/nytvr.

Nielsen, R. (2015). Introduction: The uncertain future of local journalism. In R. K. Nielsen (Ed.), *Local Journalism: The Decline of Newspapers and the Rise of Digital Media* (pp. 1–22). Oxford: Reuters Institute for the Study of Journalism.

Nikunen, K. (2016). Hopes of hospitality: Media, refugee crisis and the politics of a place. *International Journal of Cultural Studies,* 19(2), 161–176.

References 119

Noble, S. U. (2018). *Algorithms of Oppression: How Search Engines Reinforce Racism*. New York: New York University Press.

Nohrstedt, S. A., Kaitatzi-Whitlock, S., Ottosen, R., & Riegert, K. (2000). From the Persian Gulf to Kosovo: War journalism and propaganda. *European Journal of Communication*, 15(3), 383–404.

North, L. (2009). *The Gendered Newsroom*. New York: Hampton Press.

Nossek, H. & Berkowitz, D. (2007). Mythical work as journalistic practice in crisis. *Journalism Studies*, 7(5), 691–707.

Nyre, L., Bjørnestad, S., & Øie, K. V. (2012). Locative journalism: Designing a location-dependent news medium for smartphones. *Convergence*, 18(3), 297–314.

O'Callaghan, J. (2014, 25 September). Is your iPhone 6 plus too big? There's an app(endage) for that! *The Daily Mail*. Accessed 23 April 2018 at www.dailymail.co.uk/sciencetech/article-2768236/Is-iPhone-6-Plus-TOO-big-There-s-app-endage-Thumb-extender-helps-reach-screen-one-hand.html.

Oldfather, P. & West, J. (1995). Pooled case comparison: An innovation for cross-case study. *Qualitative Inquiry*, 1(4), 452–464.

Oppegaard, B. & Rabby, M. K. (2016). Proximity: Revealing new mobile meanings of a traditional news concept. *Digital Journalism*, 4(5), 621–638.

Otarola, M. & Covington, H. (2018, 3 March). More Twin Cities suburbs saying "yes" to neighbourhoods. *Star Tribune*. Accessed 23 April 2018 at www.startribune.com/more-suburbs-saying-yes-to-neighborhoods/475741163.

Pantii, M. (2010). The value of emption: An examination of television journalists' notions on emotionality. *European Journal of Communication*, 25(2), 168–181.

Papastergiadis, N. (1998). *Dialogues in the Diasporas*. London: Rivers Oram Press.

Park, R. (1922). *The Immigrant Press and Its Control*. New York: Harper and Brothers.

Park, R. (1926). The concept of position in sociology. Papers and proceedings of the American Sociological Society, University of Chicago, Chicago. Accessed at https://brocku.ca/MeadProject/Park/Park_1926a.html.

Pauli, H. (2017, 8 August). Why I quit: Local newspapers can needlessly ruin lives for empty clicks. *The Guardian*. Accessed 23 April 2018 at www.theguardian.com/media/2017/aug/08/local-news-crime-reporting-quitting-journalism.

Pavlik, J. (2013). Innovation and the future of journalism. *Digital Journalism*, 1(2), 181–193.

Peiser, J. (2018, 3 February). How a crowdsourced list set of months of #MeToo debate. *The New York Times*. Accessed 23 April 2018 at www.nytimes.com/2018/02/03/business/media/media-men-list.html.

Pertierra, A. C. (2018). *Media Anthropology for the Digital Age*. Cambridge & Medford, MA: Polity Press.

Peters, C. (2015). Introduction: The places and spaces of news production. *Journalism Studies*, 16(1), 1–11.

Peters, C. & Broersma, M. (2017). *Rethinking Journalism Again: Societal Role and Public Relevance in a Digital Age*. New York: Routledge.

Petersen, J., Sack, D., & Gabler, R. (2017). *Physical Geography*. Boston: Cengage.

Phillips, A. (2012). Sociability, speed and quality in the changing news environment. *Journalism Practice*, 6(5–6), 669–679.

120   References

Primo, A. & Zago, G. (2015). Who and what do journalism?: An actor-network perspective. *Digital Journalism*, 3(1), 38–52.

Putnam, R. (2000). *Bowling Alone: The Collapse and Revival of American Community*. New York: Simon & Schuster.

Reese, S. (2017). The new geographies of journalism research: Levels and spaces. *Digital Journalism*, 4(7), 816–826.

Richards, I. (2013). Beyond city limits: Regional journalism and social capital. *Journalism*, 14(5), 627–642.

Ricoeur, P. (1992). *Oneself as Another*. Chicago: Chicago University Press.

Rielly, C. (2016, 14 January). Why you can't have everything: The Netflix licensing dilemma. *C/net*. Accessed 23 April 2018 at www.cnet.com/news/why-you-cant-have-everything-the-netflix-licensing-dilemma.

Ritivoi, A. (2006). *Paul Ricoeur: Traditional and Innovation in Rhetorical Theory*. Albany, NY: State University of New York Press.

Roberts, H. & Sachdeva, C. (2017, 27 January). From slumdog to Hollywood: Incredible rags to riches story of Indian boy. *Daily Mail*. Accessed 23 April 2018 at www.dailymail.co.uk/news/article-4161422/From-slumdog-Hollywood-Sunny-Pawar-8-star-Lion.html.

Rothenbuhler, E. & Coman, M. (2005). *Media Anthropology*. Thousand Oaks, CA, London, & New Dehli: Sage.

Ruiz-Grossman, S. (2018, 22 February). We need to talk about black lives and gun violence after the Florida shooting. *HuffingtonPost*. Accessed 23 April 2018 at www.huffingtonpost.co.uk/entry/black-lives-gun-violence-florida-shooting_us_5a8f1a11e4b00804dfe6a466.

Said, E. W. (1979). *Culture and Imperialism*. New York: Vintage Books.

Salovaara, I. (2016). Participatory maps: Digital cartographies and the new ecology of journalism. *Digital Journalism*, 7(7), 827–837.

Sauer, C. (1925). The morphology of landscape. In J. Leighly (Ed.), *Land and Life: A Selection from the Writing of Carl Otwin Sauer* (pp. 315–359). Los Angeles: University of California Press.

Scannell, P. (1996). *Radio, Television and Modern Life*. Oxford: Blackwell.

Schmich, M. (2018, 25 January). Taking notice of Tribune Tower. *Chicago Tribune*. Accessed 23 April 2017 at www.chicagotribune.com/news/columnists/schmich/ct-met-schmich-tribune-tower-20180125-story.html.

Schmidt, C. (2018, 19 March). Whereby Us adds two more cities to its growing roster. *NiemanLab*. Accessed 23 April 2018 at www.niemanlab.org/2018/03/live-life-like-a-local-whereby-us-adds-two-more-cities-to-its-growing-roster.

Schmitz Weiss, A. (2015). Place-based knowledge in the 21st century: The creation of spatial journalism. *Digital Journalism*, 3(1), 116–131.

Schneider, N. (2012). Sourcing homelessness: How journalists use sources to frame homelessness. *Journalism*, 13(1), 71–86.

Schragger, R. (2016). *City Power: Urban Governance in a Global Age*. New York: Oxford University Press.

Scott, E. (2018, 13 January). In defense of Trump's "shithole countries" comment, his surrogates involve the "model minority" myth. *The Washington Post*. Accessed

References 121

12 April 2018 at www.washingtonpost.com/news/the-fix/wp/2018/01/13/in-defense-of-trumps-shithole-countries-comment-his-surrogates-invoke-the-model-minority-myth/?utm_term=.0a305c2159d6.

Shapley, L. (2013, 3 June). Sneak peek: Back surgery and the "breakfast test". *Denverpost.com*. Accessed 3 April 2018 at http://blogs.denverpost.com/editors/2013/06/03/back-surgery-breakfast-tes/1129.

Shoemaker, P., Lee, J. H., Gang, K., & Cohen, A. (2007). *Proximity and Scope as News Values*. In E. Devereaux (Ed.), *Media Studies: Key Issues and Debates* (pp. 231–248). London: Sage.

Shoemaker, P. & Reese, S. (2014). *Mediating the Message in the 21st Century*. New York: Routledge.

Shumow, M. & Gutsche, Jr., R. E. (2016). *News, Neoliberalism, and Miami's Fragmented Urban Space*. Lanham, MA: Lexington.

Silverstone, R. (2007). *Media and Morality: On the Rise of the Mediapolis*. London: Polity Press.

Simanowski, R. (2016). *Data Love: The Seduction and Betrayal of Digital Technologies*. New York & Chichester, West Sussex: Columbia University Press.

Soja, E. W. (2010). *Seeking Spatial Justice*. Minneapolis, MN: University of Minnesota Press.

Solon, O. (2017, 10 October). Zuckerberg tours Puerto Rico in bizarre VR promo. *The Guardian*. Accessed 23 April 2018 at www.theguardian.com/technology/2017/oct/09/mark-zuckerberg-facebook-puerto-rico-virtual-reality.

Sparks, C. (2000). Dead trees to live wires. In J.Curran & M. Gurevitch (Eds.), *Mass Media and Society* (pp. 268–292). New York: Oxford University Press.

Staines, J. (2015). *Youth Justice*. London: Palgrave MacMillan.

Steinmetz, G. (2006). Bourdieu's disavowal of Lacan: Psychoanalytic theory and the concepts of habitus and symbolic capital. *Constellations*, 13(4), 445–464.

Tang, L. & Yang, P. (2011). Symbolic power and the Internet: The power of a horse. *Media Culture Society*, 33(5), 675–691.

Taylor, A. (2018a, 13 January). Ghanaian president to Trump: We are not a "shithole country". *The Washington Post*. Accessed 23 April 2018 at www.washingtonpost.com/news/worldviews/wp/2018/01/13/ghanaian-president-to-trump-we-are-not-a-shithole-country/?utm_term=.248f6b549ad3.

Taylor, A. (2018b, 21 September). How Namibia responded to Trump inventing a country called "Nambia". *The Washington Post*. Accessed 23 April 2018 at www.washingtonpost.com/news/worldviews/wp/2017/09/21/how-namibia-responded-to-trump-inventing-a-country-called-nambia/?utm_term=.458b8b1c1d83.

Thrift, N. (2007). Immaculate warfare?: The spatial politics of extreme violence. In D. Gregory & A. Pred (Eds.), *Violent Geographies: Fear, Terror, and Political Violence* (pp. 273–294). New York & London: Routledge.

Tuan, Y. (1977). *Space and Place: The Perspective of Experience*. Minneapolis, MN: University of Minnesota Press.

Turner, V. W. (1988). *The Anthropology of Performance*. New York: PAJ Publications.

Tuzcu, P. (2016). "Allow access to location?": Digital feminist geographies. *Feminist Media Studies*, 16(1), 150–163.

122 References

Usher, N. (2018a). Considering trust: Mainstream journalism's authority problem. *Journalism Studies*, 19(4), 564–578.

Usher, N. (2018b). Breaking news production processes in US metropolitan newspapers. *Journalism*, 19(1), 21–36.

Vega, N. (2017, 1 May). We asked a hand surgeon how to treat "texting thumb". *Business Insider*. Accessed 23 April 2018 at www.businessinsider.com.au/texting-thumb-pain-what-it-is-and-how-to-treat-it-2017-4?r=US&IR=T.

Wahl-Jorgensen, K. (2010). News production, ethnography and power: On the challenges of newsroom-centricity. In S. E. Bird (Ed.), *The Anthropology of News and Journalism: Global Perspectives* (pp. 21–34). Bloomington: Indiana University Press.

Wahl-Jorgensen, K. (2013). The strategic ritual of emotionality: The case study of Pulitzer Prize-winning articles. *Journalism*, 14(1), 129–145.

Waller, L. & Hess, K. (2011). The pillory effect: Media the courts and he punitive role of public shaming in Australia. *Media Arts Law Review*, 16(3), 229–240.

Warrnambool Buy Sell Swap. (2018, 5 March). Warrnambool Buy Sell Swap Facebook page. Accessed 25 April 2018 at www.facebook.com/groups/856928164328156/about.

Weber, M. (2008). Insult to injury: The disappearance of public notices in US newspapers. *Funding the News Project*. Accessed at https://fundingthenews.usc.edu/files/2015/07/6_Carnegie_PublicNotice.pdf.

Westlund, O. (2013). Mobile news: A review and model of journalism in an age of mobile media. *Digital Journalism*, 1(1), 6–26.

Williams, A., Harte, D., & Turner, J. (2014). The value of UK hyperlocal community news: Findings from a content analysis, an online survey and interviews with producers. *Digital Journalism*, 3(5), 680–703.

Williams, R. (1976). *The Country and the City*. New York: Oxford University Press.

Williams, R. (1983). *Keywords: A Vocabulary of Culture and Society*. New York: Oxford University Press.

Winner, L. (1986). *The Whale and the Reactor: A Search for Limits in an Age of High Technology*. Chicago & London: University of Chicago Press.

Xu, V. Z. & Xiao, B. (2018, 2 April). China's social credit system seeks to assign citizen scores, engineer social behavior. *ABC*. Accessed 12 April 2018 at www.abc.net.au/news/2018-03-31/chinas-social-credit-system-punishes-untrustworthy-citizens/9596204.

Yangpen, Z. (2017, 5 September). Beijing's well to do angry as housing law forces them to mingle with poorer neighbours. *South China Morning Post*. Accessed 23 April 2018 at www.scmp.com/business/china-business/article/2109698/beijings-well-do-angry-housing-law-forces-them-mingle-poorer.

Yanich, D. (2005). Location, location, location: Urban and suburban crime on local TV news. *Journal of Urban Affairs*, 23(3–4), 221–241.

Zelizer, B. (1990). Where is the author in American TV news?: On the construction and presentation of proximity, authorship and journalistic authority. *Semiotica*, 80, 37–48.

Zonn, L. (1990). *Place Images in Media: Portrayal, Experience, and Meaning*. Savage, MD: Rowman & Littlefield.

Index

Aboriginal Australians, historical portrayal 99
Adams, Paul 15, 106
"affective geographies" 106
Ahva and Pantii: forms of proximity as they relate to journalism 68–9; importance of audience proximity 78; social-ideological proximity 69, 70
Amish country murder, portrayal 44–5
Anderson, Benedict 48, 77, 104
Arkansas floods, largely ignored by big media 17–18
audience-centred approaches to news 106
audience expectations: interpreting geography through 64–6; Tulsa, Oklahoma 64–5
audience proximity, importance for news outlets 78
audiences: in the digital age 104–5, 107–8; for journalistic legitimacy 64, 88; and perceptions of journalistic proximity to place 6, 69, 77–9
Australian Broadcasting Corporation (ABC) 10
Australian Communications and Media Authority 33, 55
autonomous temporality 76; and journalism practices 77–8
"awayness" 95–6

banishment: of undesirables 96, 106; via boosterism 96
Beijing, China, affluent homeowners, and community 39–40
Biden, Joe 72

birth notices 28
black communities, physical and ideological violence in 82–3
black residents, Iowa, doxic attitudes 43
Bloomington, Minnesota, negotiating new boundaries 52, 53
borders: and boundaries 102, 103–4; mapping of movement at and across 106
boundary maintenance 29
boundary work 3, 6, 30, 38, 96, 104; and ritual in place-making 45–6; used to explore how journalists cement their professional standing from others 45
Bourdieu, Pierre 50; concept of "site effects" 74; and journalistic legitimacy 41; notion of symbolic power 5, 38, 39; symbolic misrecognition 72; symbolic violence 42
Bourdieusian notion of "doxa" 38
"breakfast test" 80
breaking news 76–7
bridging geographic divides through narratives of oppression 97–9
Brierley, Saroo 1
broadband services, impact of poor quality access to 9–10
broadcasting boundaries 12
Bruns, Axel 50
bushfires 9–10, 40

Cambridge Analytica scandal 31, 91
Carey, James 95; ritual analysis 46
Castells, Manuel 24, 25

124   Index

Chicago, Illinois, as centre of cultural, political and economic capital 58
Chicago Tribune 58
China's social credit ratings system 92–3
cities: Chicago, Illinois 58; interpreting geography through audience expectations, Tulsa, Oklahoma 64–6; mythical archetypes of good and evil deployed in news coverage of 14, 44–5; negotiating new boundaries, Bloomington, Minnesota 52, 53; residents' right to the city 96; WhereBy.Us affiliates, digital stories 88–9
citizen journalism 60, 104
city-making campaigns 96
city/rural divide 13, 41–2; in readers' perceptions of state news media 57
classical landscape studies 13
closed communities online 14
Columbine High school killings 48
commercial broadcasting licenses 55
communication: as a form of violence against difference and diversity 96; ritual of 95
communications technology, and trivialisation of concept of "place" 9
community: and bushfires 9–10, 40; and geographic territory 39–40; journalists selection of quotes to reflect the 40–1; mythical archetypes to portray characters of small communities 44–5; and news media power over 34; power of 35–6; and racial discrimination 43; sense of, and Facebook's local "I love my town" sites 34; as synonymous with physical places 11
cosmopolitanism 46, 79–80
Costera Maijer, Irene 106
Couldry, Nick 46, 75
court rooms: and court reporting 73; as sites of symbolic power 74
Craddock, Mike 65
crisis reporting 17
critical and cultural geography 8
critical geographic studies 6
cultural anthropology 20n.4
cultural binaries 14, 29, 41, 45, 103

cultural capital 60, 75, 79
cultural geography 11, 103, 105; and landscape studies 13–14; and meaning-making function of locations 12; media and the material turn in 14–16; and ongoing relationship to other people and places 14; where control and communication collide 12–13
cultural interpretations of geographies 20n.5
cultural "landscape", changing nature of 13–14
cultural studies 13

dangers of unfamiliarity of geography and place experiences 81–2
data manipulators 87
data visualisation 86
Dear, Michael 105
death notices 27–8
demarcating news spaces in digital news 5–6, 52–66
digital age: audiences in the 104–5, 107–8; journalism practice and its relationship to place in 104; journalism's place in the 3; journalists as place-makers in the 109
digital distraction 85–8; definition 85; and digital technologies 85; and empowerment of types of "journalistic evidence" 87; and indoctrination through passive acceptance of new ways of storytelling 85–6; via seduction to success measures 88–91
digital divide 9
digital geographies 20n.6; influence on widening audiences 107–8
digital journalism 84–101, 108–9; directs users to what is "popular" and "appropriate" 106; and growing the number of subscribers 89–90; and "innovative" approaches to "doing news" 90; meaning-making "made" through data visualisation, interactive charts and maps 86; measures of success 88–91; mobility of 104; and "place" 15; Poynter article on 89–90; trichotomy of place, space and territory 5, 21–37

Index 125

digital media tools, use of 21–2
digital news, demarcating news spaces in 5–6, 52–66
digital newswork, hiding place-making in 85–8
digital public sphere, as territory 29–31
digital space: as democratizing force 75; mythical archetypes of good and evil deployed in news coverage of 14; as "places" of meaning for audiences 28; and problems of funeral notices not being "in their usual place" 28; proximity to power 74–6; and resurging interest in journalism studies toward the material 15; and territory 28–9
digital surveillance 91–2; and China's social credit ratings system 92
digital technologies: and digital distraction 85; and journalism's "success" 89; and journalistic control 87; journalists influenced by 90–1; and the "seduction" of evidence 86; to get a "feel for a place" 26; to map events 86, 97–8
distance, role in journalistic place-making 59–60
"distant sufferers" 80
"Downstate" Illinois: definition 56; Facebook discussion of terminology surrounding "Downstate" 56–7; process of place-demarcation 55, 56–9
"Downtown" Tulsa, Oklahoma, audience expectations of geography 64–6
doxa: Bourdieusian notion 38; definition 39; and imagination 51n.6; importance to geographies of journalism 39
doxic ideas 45; about homelessness 71–2; of "community" 40, 43; of professional journalists 30, 41–2, 43–4, 49, 100n.1; reinforcement, Salem, Oregon 61–4

"electronic landscapes" 14
elites: as custodians of civic virtue 40–1; as drivers of imaginative power 48–9; with symbolic power demarcate dominant boundaries 53

embodied knowledge of places 79
emotive responses 46–7
environmental journalism 9
ethics 80
ethnic print newspapers 11
"eyewitness" reporting 97

Facebook 10, 17, 23, 26, 86; "community" 36; data breaches and invasion of privacy 76, 91; dominance in the social sphere 31; "Downstate" terminology discussion 56–7; foundations 30; and Harvard University 35; local "I love my town" sites 34; and news media 29, 31–2; not an agent of the public sphere 30; not a news outlet 30; and the rise of fake news 31; and rules of space 35–6; selling private data for political purposes 31, 81; strategy to build territory in digital spaces 35; "tasteless" VR video of Puerto Rican floods 18; use of emotional tactics in constructing its boundaries 47
fake news 31, 91
federal courts of law, as sites of symbolic and economic power 74
Feik, Nick 31
filter bubbles 3, 90–1
fixers 80–1
"Flat Earth" approach to geography studies 7
"Flat Earth News" 7
flooding: Arkansas, ignored by big media 17–18; Puerto Rico, Zuckerberg's VR broadcast criticized 18
fourth estate 30, 78
funeral notices 28

Garnett newspapers 61
gendered meanings of "city" and "country" 13
geo-social journalism 7, 8; to understand local media 7
geo-spatial tools 15–16; for reporting natural disasters 17
geographic terrain, and information and communication "blackspots" 9
geographic territory 104; and community 39–40

126 *Index*

geographic wayfinding 105
geographies of journalism 4–5;
advancing the research agenda 102–9;
mapping 7–19
geography: definition 8; and
journalism 4, 8
geography studies: and its relevance
to journalism 7–19; in Western
contexts 4–5
Global Reporting Center, on journalist-
fixer relationships 81
Goffman's dramaturgical observations
of frontstage behavior 73, 75
Goldberg, Susan 98
Google: "Propensity to Subscribe"
technology 91–2; sharing data with
authoritative sources 75
Google algorithms: as a global system
of totalitarianism 76; promoting
"authoritative" sources in search
engine results 75
Google Maps 26
government advertising spending 33
governments: legitimising power 73;
and media 33
Graham, Ginnie 65
gun violence, international protest
against 82–3
Gutsche, Jr., Robert: "digital
distraction" 85; "journalistic
evidence" 86; souseveillance 93

Harvard University, and Facebook 35
Hedges, Chris 75–6
hegemonic dominant perspectives 5,
49, 53, 99
Herwig, Jana 36
Hess, Kristy, and journalistic
legitimacy 41
Hollywood actresses, sexual abuse 49
homelessness 70–2; "experts'" voices
72; and proximity to power 72; and
"sense of place" 70–1; story, *Tampa
Bay Times* 71–2
"homogeneous empty time" 77
homogeneous temporal proximity 76
human geography 8
human impacts on natural landscape, as
manifestation of culture 13
humanitarian issues, reporting on 80

"I love my town" Facebook sites 34
Illinois, place-demarcation based on
distribution of power and social
capital 55, 56–9
imaginary and imagination,
constructs 48
imagination: and doxa 51n.6; and
symbolic power 48–9
"imaginative community" 48, 104
"imaginative" notion of place 38
"imaginative power" 5, 38, 48; definition
47; driven by elites 48–9; of the press
48; and symbolic power 47
"imaginative power of place" 5; in
journalism studies 47–9, 50–1
imagined audience 2, 82
"immersive journalism" 15
Indians, denied access to US 1
indoctrinated observation via news
coverage 86
information and communication
blackspots 9, 10
information inequality based on
geography and distance from centres
of power 9–10
informational inequalities, rural and
regional communities 9–10
innovation, and journalism studies
scholarship 50
institutions of power, news media
dependence on to shape territorial
boundaries 29, 32–3
international journalists 80; relationship
with fixers 81; use of fixers 80–1
"international news" 80
internet, recognizing the value of
legitimate journalism 75
investigative journalism 49
"invisibilization" of individuals or
groups 42–4

Jaffe, Logan 56–7, 59
jigsaw puzzles, place-based 67–8
journalism: in the 21st century 23–4; in
the changing media environment 47–9;
and the city/country divide 13, 41–2;
and emotional responses 47; and
Facebook 31–2; and the imagination
of boundaries 103–4; innovative role
in rethinking social justice issues 59;

Index 127

and materiality 15–16; "place" in the digital age 3; and place-making 2, 15, 16; professional, as doxa 41–2, 43–5, 49; in the public sphere 2; re-imagining a role for 49–51; relationship to place-making 2, 5, 15, 16, 52–3, 78; "serving" communities 99; and social media 11, 36, 104; in the social sphere 2–3; spatial dialectic of 95–7; symbolic and imaginative power 38–51; trichotomy of place, space and territory 21–37

journalism practice: and its relationship to place in the digital age 104; as a social and cultural process of power 91; and watchdogging of private citizens 91

journalism rituals, changes in covering place 82, 83

journalism studies: "imaginative power of place" in 47–9, 50–1; lack of reflexivity in 50; and physical geography 9

journalism studies scholarship, and innovation 50

journalist-fixer relationship 81

journalistic authority, promotion of through technological tricks 74

"journalistic awareness" 98

journalistic control, and digital technologies 87

"journalistic evidence" 86

journalistic legitimacy 41, 52, 104; location and proximity crucial for promotion of 74; through audiences 64, 88

journalistic place-making, role of distance 59–60

journalistic processes of place-shaming 93–5

journalistic productivity, and demarcation of zones 60

journalistic proximity to place 97; audience and perceptions of 6, 69, 77–9; threats to in small-town media 79

journalistic reflexivity 50, 98–9; in place-making 107–9

journalistic stringers 60

journalistic success, measuring 88, 89–90

journalistic work 96

journalists: accountability 3; and breaking news updates 76–7; commitment to the public sphere 30–1; complain that Facebook is not subjected to the same rules as they are 30; dangers of unfamiliarity of geography and place experiences 81–2; demarcation of spaces and border watching 53; engagement with audiences "close to them" but separated by social and/or cultural distances 70–2; importance of geographic location 79; influenced by digital technologies 90–1; interpreting geography through audience expectations 64–6; physical proximity to power 72–3; pressured by audiences and advertisers 52; professional, doxic ideas 30, 41–2, 43–5; and the Sea Level Rise App 87–8; selection of quotes to reflect the "community" view 40–1; symbolic power 73; visualization of "communities", borders and boundaries 15; work according to core values and pressures 45

journalists as place-makers 3, 4; in the digital age 109; methodological approaches 6

killing of blacks by white police, narrative explanations 98

Latour's actor network theory 16

legitimate journalism, recognizing the value of on the internet 75

Lion (film) 1–2

L.L. Bean's custom-made jigsaw puzzles of people's hometowns 67–8

local communities: and Facebook's "I love my town" sites 34; and social media 34–5

local habitas, as applied to news media and journalism 78–9

local journalists, comparison with metropolitan journalists 42, 43

local news media: and geo-social journalism 7; relationship to

128 *Index*

community-building and social capital 11–12
local newspapers: amalgamation and cultural dimensions of space 55; death and funeral notices in 27–8; digital innovation limited by poor broadband 9; don't reflect how community members feel 34; government advertising in 33; shift from print to online 27
local reporters, experiences of 42
locative journalism 7
locative news 7

McGaughy, Lauren 81–2
McLemore, Dylan 17–18
mapping and maps 7–19, 26, 86, 97–8, 106
marginalization of geography 12
mass shooting: Sutherland Springs, Texas, and onslaught of journalists 81–2, *see also* school shooting
Massey, Doreen 3, 10, 24
material dimensions of space and place 19
material objects, and "places of meaning" 14
material turn 26; in cultural geography 14–16
May, Thornton 9
measuring journalistic success in the digital realm 88, 89–90
"media anthropology" within journalism studies 107
media geography 14–15
media innovation 50
media outlets: connection to their home places 95; power and influence 3
media platforms, and society 105
media power, reinforcement of 87
media ritual 36; and boundary work in place-making 45–6; and "mediated social order" 46
media shaming 6, 93; Shenzhen, China 92
media technology, and journalism 16, 22
media territory *see* territory
mediated sense of place 26–8
"mediated social order" 46
mental mapping in journalism 106

#MeToo movement 49
metropolitan journalists: comparison with local/regional journalists 42, 43; dangers of unfamiliarity of geography and place experiences 81–2; little experience of rural issues and daily life 108; parachuted into towns when required 79, 82
Miami, The New Tropic site, digital stories 88
migration movements 106
mobile media spheres, perceptions of place in 104–7
mobile phone and internet blackspots 9, 10
moral codes 93
Morley, David 28; "electronic landscapes" 14; imagined geographies and boundaries 45; "sense of place" with death notices 27
mythical archetypes: of good and evil in urban news coverage 14, 44–5; to demarcate social and geographic positions of power 44; and undoing of Weinstein 49

narratives of oppression, to bridge geographic divides 97–9
National Geographic: early articles on issues of race within a geographic context 99; "faraway" lands viewed through mediated imperialistic and colonizing storytelling 98–9
natural disasters: importance of location, classes and cultures 17–18; and journalism 17, 18
natural world, impact on journalism practice 8–9, 16
Neiman Reports, on journalist-fixer relationship 81
Netflix 54
"network society" 24, 25, 30
The New York Times library of VR projects 77–8
news: audience-centred approaches 106; of the past, and social conditions at the time 108
news buildings, as "places" of authoritative and legitimate news production 26

Index 129

news habits 26–7
news maps 15
news media: ability to reinforce doxic
ideas such as "community" 34;
attitude to Facebook 31–2; circulation
allied with politically constructed
regions 33; constraints on "where"
they can be broadcast or published
12; construct of local habitas as it
applies to 78–9; as custodian of the
universal doxic idea of a common
good 41; and demarcation of space in
physical geography 5–6; dependence
on other institutions of power to
shape territorial boundaries 32–3;
and digital data exploitation debates
91–2; and Facebook 29, 31–2; as
free and public space for all 30; and
government advertising spending 33;
influence within the political field
22–3, 33; legitimacy in society 32;
as members of the power elite 3;
as a "place" 26–8; as place-makers
and generated perceptions of places
106; power of how they shape the
way we give meaning to places 13;
relationship to social surveillance 6;
relationship to weather 16–18; role
2, 32; shaping perception of location
2; and temporal dimensions of place
78; use of technology to connect
people with others 12; as wielders of
symbolic power 39
news media players, adopting locating
technologies to follow news users 75
news media territory 22–3, 28–9;
ability to mediate and shape
perceptions around places of
meaning 29, 34–5; at the meta-
level 29, 30; dependence on other
institutions of power 29, 32–3
news myth 14, 38; as power tool for
place-making 44–5
news outlets, importance of audience
proximity 78
news proximity 67–83; performative
proximity 6, 69, 73–4, 75, 97;
research frameworks 68–9; social-
ideological proximity 6, 69–73;
temporal proximity 6, 76–8

news users, need for familiar
environments 27
news zones: boundaries 54;
characterization of place, Salem,
Oregon 61–4; and contested space,
"Downstate" Illinois 55, 56–9;
coverage 55; cultural markers 55;
definition 54; demarcation of,
and journalistic productivity 60;
interpreting geography through
audience expectation 64–6; and
journalistic practice 55–9; in
physical and digital geographies
53–5; and role of distance in
journalistic place-making 59–60;
scale and reach 54–5
newspaper reading, and idea of
"place" 26
newspapers, and people's sense of
place 32
Newton, Grace 42
NiemanLan 88

Oklahoma City bombings 48
online shaming, Shenzhen, China 92
Oppegaard and Rabby's "place-based"
news 69
Overall, Michael 64–6

Park, Robert 11
Parkland, Florida, school shooting,
racialized connotations 82–3
"participatory" practices 60
Pate, Natalie 61–4
performative proximity 6, 69, 73–4,
97; and agents of power in political
buildings and courts 74; and
breaking news 77; in digital space
75; in theater 73
Pew Research Centre 75
physical geography: and connection to
the Earth 7, 8–9; and environmental
journalism 9; and journalism studies
9; meaning-making with our feet
on the ground 8–10; and spatial and
environmental processes 8–9; and
three-dimensional accounts of news 7
physical proximity 79–83
"place" 24–5; characterizing in the
news 61–4; news media as a 26–8;

130 *Index*

perceptions of in mobile media spheres 104–7; and "sense of place" 25–6; and "space", relationship to news media and journalism 4–5; technology's trivialisation of concept of 9
place-based jigsaw puzzles 67–8
place-based knowledge: and spatial journalism 7; within the scope of geographies of journalism 9
"place-based" news 69
place-demarcation, "Downstate" Illinois 55, 56–9
place-making: boundary work and ritual in 45–6; journalism's relationship to 2, 5, 15, 16, 52–3; journalistic reflexivity in 107–9; news myth as power tool for 44–5; power of and power inherent in 5; proximity and distance in the context of 6, 67–83
place-names in local news 79
place-shaming, journalistic processes of 93–5
places of meaning, news media's ability to mediate and shape perceptions around 34–5
political broadcast journalists, juxtaposed against parliamentary buildings 74
political buildings, as sites of symbolic and economic power 74
political geography 19n.3
politics, news media influence in 22–3, 33
pooled case comparison approach 4
power: as an ideological process 3; unification and endorsement of 75
"power geometry" 3, 24
power of community 35–6
power of territory 5
Poynter article on digital journalism 89–90
press briefing rooms: access to agents of media power 74; and locations of economic power 73
press conference, ritual of in a digital world 74
print newspapers 9
problem-solving: at the center of coverage 108; and dealing with "another's" culture 108

professional journalists, doxic ideas 30, 41–2, 43–4, 49, 100n.1
ProPublica Illinois, process of place-demarcation, "Downstate" Illinois 55, 56–9
proximity 68, 83; Ahva and Pantii's forms that relate to journalism 68–9; audience and perceptions of journalistic proximity to place 6, 69, 77–9, 97; and distance, in the context of place-making 6, 67–83; and notion of cosmopolitanism 79–80; Oppegaard and Rabby's "place-based" news 69; performative 6, 69, 73–4, 77, 97; physical 79–83; social-ideological 6, 69–72; temporal 6, 76–8
proximity to events, as crucial to promotion of journalistic authority 74
proximity to power 6; by journalists 72–4; in digital space 74–6; and homelessness 72
public sphere 30; connection with social sphere 31; digital 29–31; journalism in the 2, 30; as "territory" 29–31
Puerto Rico floods, Zuckerberg's VR broadcast criticized 18

qualitative measures 86
quantitative measures 86

race, *National Geographic* portrayals of 98–9
racial connotations, school shooting, Parkland, Florida 82–3
racial discrimination, Iowa 43
racial divide, and police violence 98
racial stratification 11
racism, influence of 97–8, 99
radio 32
reflexivity: in journalism 98–9, 107–9; in news practices, importance of 49, 50
research agenda 102–9
"right to the city" 96, 99
"right to the story" 96, 97, 100
riots, London, and the "why" of violence 97–8
rising waters, visualizing the effects of, South Florida 87
ritual communication and community 46
Rosenberg, Mike 89

Index 131

rural and regional communities: informational inequalities 9–10; largely ignored by big media 18; mobile phone and internet blackspots 10
rural reporters, experiences 42

Salem, Oregon, *Statesman Journal* 61–4
Sauer, Carl, classical landscape studies 13
school shooting, Parkland, Florida, racialized connotations 82–3
Sea Level Rise App 87
Seattle, The Evergrey site, digital stories 89
Seattle Times: on growing digital subscribers 90; "influence" project, and analytics to measure journalistic success 89–90, 92
"sense of place" 3, 24–6; funeral and death notices in local papers 27–8; and homelessness 70–1; mediated 26–8; and social groups 35–6
sexual assault and harassment in the workplace 49
shaming 6, 92–5, 96; and blaming 93, 96
"shithole" nations 84, 94
"site effects" 74
"situational geography" 9
small-town mass shooting, and onslaught of journalists 81–2
small-town media, subjected to centralization and dispersion of news resources 79
small-town reporters, experiences 42
small-town sexual violence, portrayal 44
sociability: in journalism 11; of news 11
social anthropology 20n.4
social control 92; and China's social credit system 92; through online shaming, Shenzhen, China 92
social credit system, China 92–3
social geography 10–12, 105; addressing issues of marginalization and inequalities 12; and journalism 11, 12; meaning 11; "place-matters" approach to government policies and economic restraint of media 12; and spatial organization of people 12
social groups, turning place into territory 35–6

social-ideological proximity 6, 69–72
social journalism 11
social justice 6, 50, 70–2, 96, 99
social meanings of journalism 10–12
social media 10; and connection to place 11; and increased competition for the news story first 77; and journalism 11, 36, 104; and local communities 34–5, *see also* Facebook
social media tools 11
social networking 10, 11
social networking theories 16
social sphere: connection with public sphere 31; emotions in the 47; Facebook dominance in 31; journalism in 2–3; as new contested territory 5, 31–2; news media and Facebook in 31–2
social surveillance, journalists as masters of 100n.4
socially constructed inequalities 97–9, 100, 102
"solutions journalism" 108
souseveillance 93
South Florida, visualizing the effects of rising waters 87
"space" 4–5, 24
"space of flows" 24, 25
"spaces of blaming" 93
"spaces of pain" 86
spatial dialectic 84; of journalism 95–7, 106
"spatial turn" 3, 38
spontaneous temporality 76; and authority 76–7
Statesman Journal (Salem, Oregon): coverage 61; and defined geographies, cultures and political boundaries 61–2; different approaches to reporting on schools and neighbourhoods based on location 62–3; geographic locations of spaces 61–4; as mid-sized paper 61; reinforcement of doxic attitudes in specific geographic spaces 63; reporting based on community spatial stereotypes 63
subscriptions, boosting digital 89
surveillance, digital 91–2, 93
Sutherland Springs, Texas, mass shooting, and onslaught of journalists 81–2

132 *Index*

symbolic misrecognition 72
symbolic power 5, 39, 47; Bourdieu's notion of 5, 38, 39; definition 38; of journalists 73
symbolic violence in mediated "places" 38, 42–4; legitimization 42–3

Tampa Bay Times, story on homelessness and giving 71–2
technological innovation 15
technology: and journalism practices 16, *see also* digital technologies
television 32
temporal proximity 6, 76–8
territory: and battles in the social sphere 5, 31–3; connection with media 22–3; connection with place 23; digital public sphere as 29–31; as the missing element in journalism studies 22–3; news media dependence on other institutions of power to shape 32–3; and news media's ability to mediate and shape perceptions around places of meaning 34–5; power of 5; and social groups 35–6; spaces and places of journalism 23–6; unpacking 28–9
"texting thumb" 21, 22
theater, performance proximity 73
"there", covering places of 80
"time-space compression" 23, 24, 77
Tow Center for Digital Journalism 78
Tribune Tower, Chicago, name change 58–9
trichotomy of place, space and territory 5, 21–37
Trump, Donald 31, 57, 73; disdain for countries other than his own 84, 94–5; plan for a wall along US/Mexico border 103, 104
Tulsa, Oklahoma, challenge of meeting the audience expectations of geography 64–6

Tulsa World 64–6
Twitter 32

United States/Mexican border 103, 104; local media role 105
urban sprawl, and challenges of social cohesion and collective identity 52
urban studies 5–6, 11–12
Usher, Nikki 26

violence by white police, and racial divide 98
violence of riots, linked to "realities" of class and race struggles 97–8
virtual proximity 68
virtual reality (VR): challenging core journalistic questions 78; *New York Times* library of 77–8; and power dimension between audience and journalism 78; and power of place-making 18; Zuckerberg criticized for use of VR showing Puerto Rican floods 18

weather: importance of in our daily lives 17; and natural disasters 18; and news media 16–18
Weinstein affair, portrayal of 49
"where" of news 80
WhereBy.Us newsletters and stories 88
White House press briefings 73
wild weather 17
Williams, Raymond 13
Winner, Langdon 90
Wozniak, Steve 76

Zuckerberg, Mark: criticized for his "tasteless" VR video of Puerto Rican floods 18; Facebook and Harvard University 35; Facebook creation 29; on Facebook's data breaches and invasion of privacy 91